CARDIAC CHAMPS

A Survivor's Guide

How to Live a Healthy, Vigorous, Happy Life After a Heart Attack

Dr. Larry McConnell

Cardiac Champs is not intended as personal health, medical or psychological advice. Readers should consult their own professional advisor(s) before adopting any of the suggestions in this book. The opinions and viewpoints expressed are solely those of the author.

First Edition 2010
ISBN 9781450512084
Photograph on back cover by Katherine Caine

For Sharon, Jude, and Lucas
My Heroes

Acknowledgements

This book has been a work in progress for over a decade. I want to thank Wilda Ryckman for her assistance in preparing the initial draft. I am also grateful to Phyllis Hodges for sharing her expertise on nutrition and for providing her tough, but effective, critical analysis during the preparation of the manuscript. A special word of thanks to Dr. Katherine Caine, my favourite psychologist. Her sage advice is reflected throughout the book.

It was the dedicated work of my dear wife, Sharon Mulroney, that finally moved my material from the drawing board to publication. She served as technical advisor, researcher, cheerleader and editor-in-chief throughout the project. I remain in awe of 'Big Shar's' amazing skill set which includes advanced research methods, refined problem-solving abilities and the capacity to consistently generate innovative solutions for an endless number of complex technical issues. These professional traits combined with her beauty, sense of humour, and love of sports make it clear why I am the luckiest guy on the planet.

I also extend a big thank you to my sons, Jude and Lucas, who have enriched my life in more ways than I could ever express in words. I continue to marvel at their capacity for independent thought, sound judgment, good humour and care for each other.

Finally, a word of thanks to my golfing buddies. Our golf games are the only medicine I use and it obviously works.

Contents

Preface

The Beat Goes On!

The evening of Thursday, December 9, 1982, is permanently engraved on my mind. That night I played my last game of competitive ice hockey. Actually the game was uneventful until the last few minutes of the third period. That is when I took a heart attack. Imagine, the big one at thirty-eight years old. That has to rate in the top ten for midlife crises, but it is not the ultimate. I was saving that experience for my forties.

You have a heart attack at a young age; you make a few changes. I gave up smoking, reduced my fat intake, stopped playing competitive hockey, diligently followed a moderate exercise program, and learned to worry a lot. It wasn't enough. On August 11, 1985, I took my second heart attack. This time it was a double feature. Heart attack and cardiac arrest. The ultimate midlife crisis at forty-one years old. My life had changed forever!

Most people thought I was a fairly regular guy before my heart attacks. I was happily married with a couple of toddlers and looking forward to starting a new job in a new city where I was going to further my professional career. I regularly ran five to ten kilometres with relative ease, played a good brand of competitive hockey and was tough at tennis. I had never experienced any health problems. In fact, it was rare for me to even get a cold. I did smoke nearly a pack of cigarettes a day, but I had been doing that with no ill effects for over twenty years. I was a moderate drinker with a good appetite, although I ate a lot of fried foods with my fruits and vegetables. I was aggressive, very competitive, and had my share of anger, impatience, persistence and sensitivity floating around my psyche. I also had, and continue to have, a hell of a sense of humour. Maybe this profile isn't a health promoter's dream, but who would have thought it was a passport to living hell? It was. However, things began to change for me a few years after my last brush with death. The result? It is now twenty-five years since my last heart attack, and I am still living a happy, healthy, vigorous life.

I am a retired psychologist. I graduated with a doctoral degree from McGill University in 1975 and have practiced the trade in Quebec, Alberta and British Columbia, Canada. My training and experience in counselling psychology certainly helps me to better understand the plight of a cardiac survivor. However, that understanding has been vastly enriched by personally confronting the pain and challenge one has to face following a heart attack. This medical history combined with my academic background leaves me in the unique position of being able to view the struggle for survival from a professional and personal perspective.

Cardiac Champs has been written with an overriding objective in mind.....to help people with heart disease, particularly heart attack survivors, find peace and contentment. I believe it is possible for people, young or old, to live a meaningful and happy life with heart disease, even after a heart attack. This doesn't necessarily mean you will get a clean bill of health from a cardiologist or family physician. It means being glad you are alive, feeling good, feeling in charge of your life and not perpetually worrying about when you are going to die. You can experience this state of well-being even with angina or after two or three heart attacks, cardiac arrest, by-pass surgery, or a valve job.

No doubt much of what I have written, if applied, can help prevent heart disease. However, it is not so much about prevention as survival. I can hardly tout myself as an expert on prevention. After all, I had two heart attacks and a cardiac arrest before the

ii

age of forty-two. But I do see myself as pretty much of an expert on survival. I guess some people would say I am just plain lucky, but I don't think so. Sure, luck plays a part, as do genes, but that is far from the whole story. My survival is more about how I came to grips with the reality that my life was a time bomb.

The journey to healthy, happy living is a long one, and it can be a particularly lonely one after a heart attack. However, it need not be so lonely if the helpers of the world better understood the challenges facing the cardiac survivor. This is why I also wish to share my thoughts with the many caregivers who try to help heart attack survivors. Here I speak of the nurses, physicians, rehabilitation counsellors, families and friends of heart attack survivors. I want to help them to better understand the anguish survivors must overcome on their journey toward happy living. It is so important for friends and helpers to understand their plight.

Cardiac Champs has also been written for those brave people who have survived heart surgery, those suffering with the misery of angina, and those who have been diagnosed with any other kind of heart disease. This book is for you too, but it is not a book on how to live your life. Rather the book is designed to help you ensure that the condition of your arteries and heart do not completely dictate the kind of life you live. Most of all, this book is about hope because it is written by a person who, twenty-five years later, is still living a healthy, vigorous and happy life even though he suffered two heart attacks and experienced cardiac arrest for a few moments.

The beat goes on!

I
The Witch Doctors' Hotel

It is not easy to sit in a hospital waiting room wondering if someone you love is going to die any minute. That is why I hope this book is on a coffee table in the waiting room, or there is a nurse or physician around who has it. It could be helpful to read some of it now. Heart attacks are not only tough on the victim. They scare the hell out of the loved ones, particularly the spouse. So I thought I would start with a few words to you.......the forgotten people who are worrying in hospital waiting rooms.

The Waiting Room Blues

Now that your partner is in the hospital alive, the chances of survival are pretty good. In fact, in a month or two things will probably be getting back to normal. I know, right now it is hard to believe your life will ever be normal again. How can it be after a heart attack? Actually, in one way you are right. When someone dear to you has a heart attack or any other serious heart problem, it is bound to have a lasting effect on your life. However, you haven't been sentenced to a life of misery. Your sense of optimism will quickly return as you witness your loved one's progress.

> **Cardiac Survivors Haven't Been
> Handed A Death Sentence
> So Don't Treat Them Like
> The Walking Dead**

During the early stages of recovery, cardiac survivors need the help of professionals such as nurses, physicians and counsellors. However, it is the help and support from their loved ones that serve them best over the long haul. So you have a real challenge before you, but you can meet it. This book is primarily directed at the person with the heart problems, but I am confident it will also prove helpful to you. It can give you a clearer understanding of the trials and tribulations your friend or partner will face as a cardiac survivor. I talk about the hospital stay, getting home and returning to work. I also talk about nutrition, exercise and learning how to avoid spending the rest of your days worrying about the next heart attack. Most of these subjects are very important to the survivor, so you will feel better if you also know about them. A little knowledge can help you cope better. However, right now you are probably most concerned about the next couple of hours, so why don't we look in on your survivor.

The M.A.S.H. Attack

A heart attack gets attention. It really does freak people out. You have probably already learned there is nothing other than near fatal accidents that can crank up the medical establishment more than heart attacks. It is no exaggeration to say that your loved one has embarked on a vastly new experience where he or she will witness the medical world at its most intense. This can be a real shocker if you have no previous experience dealing with the medical system. However, like it or not, your friend or partner will be the centre of attention for at least the next forty-eight hours. It may well prove to be an awesome experience, but it is a necessary one.

Most heart attack victims arrive at the hospital in a serious state. They may be feeling incredibly weak, experiencing chest pains, or even unconscious. Regardless, their first stop is the emergency ward. In modern hospitals the emergency ward has the staff and equipment required to handle the wildest medical crisis, but the medical team must work fast. So don't feel insulted if you are just shunted aside. The physicians and nurses will work around you. They may even suggest that you go hang out in the waiting room. The staff in an emergency ward work a lot in overdrive and are not necessarily experts in human relations. At this point their job is to diagnose and stabilize your mate. They are concerned with the most complicated workings of the victim's cardiovascular system, as well as the more mundane aspects such as heart beat, blood pressure and level of pain. This can be a scary time for the victim, but don't worry. There is a good chance some nurse close by will have a sense of the occasion and whisper words of reassurance to the patient. The pain? Most physicians manage the victim's pain with generous doses of morphine. I can tell you from experience, after a few shots of that stuff, the world feels pretty dandy. It is not hard to understand why it is such an addictive drug.

Sometimes people with serious heart problems go into cardiac arrest. This is where the heart stops pumping blood. It is as though the required electrical current short circuits in the system. If nothing is done quickly, the victim dies. The heart is acting like a dead battery in a car, so it needs a boost. Electrical conductors are attached to the body and the heart is given an electrical jolt to get it beating again. This all sounds very gruesome, but the patient is unaware of the events. Once their heart stops they pass out and don't perceive anything that happens until they return to a conscious state. They may have a few sore muscles depending on the intensity of the shocks, but there are no long term aftereffects.

The Spook House
Once your mate is stabilized, the next stop is the Intensive Care Unit (ICU). This is a spooky looking place, especially when the lights are dim and everybody whispers. A bit like a funeral parlour except the star of the show blinks. Nevertheless, it is a safe place. In the ICU patients receive very personalized care. They are usually

hooked up to a couple of machines. In all likelihood, they will also have electrodes attached to their chests. These pick up body signals that are registered on the monitoring machines. The monitors allow the nurses to follow the heart beat and rhythms from their station in the hall. One of the machines even has an alarm that will sound if anything goes wrong. Oh ya, that hanging bottle with a needle attached to the back of the hand is intravenous. It is just pumping a little energy into your survivor's body.

The Intensive Care Unit is exactly what the name suggests: the patient receives intensive care from the nurses and physicians. However, some small hospitals don't have a special ICU, so the patient is moved directly from emergency to a general ward. Alternatively, some of the bigger hospitals have large cardiac wards that include their own intensive care unit. In any event, your partner will probably be on a regular ward within a couple of days.

Once the survivor's condition has stabilized, you will be allowed to see them even if they are in intensive care. Note, I used the word 'allowed'. One thing you will quickly discover with the medical establishment....they are take charge types who like to run the hospital like a school. The MDs are the principals, the nurses the teachers, and everyone else is a student. Anyway, a visit as soon as possible is the best thing for both of you. Let me tell you a little something about the person lying in the bed. It is in the ICU that they will start to realize what has happened to them. At this point, one emotion dominates.....fear! So don't get too excited about anything your partner says at this time. People don't always think in the most rational way when they are afraid.

So what do I do now? I think there are a few basics that just about everyone needs right after a heart attack. First, they need someone they love close by them. They also need to hear that they are going to be all right, and most people need a little bit of the mushy stuff. Many heart attack victims, especially men, are aggressive, independent types with a low tolerance level for cry babies. That was then; this is now.

> ## Crying Doesn't Cause Stress
> ## It Reduces It

It is a good time to hold hands and quietly share your feelings of fear. The guy, or gal, just had a heart attack. There is going to be a little fear in the air. The ol' sucker is really vulnerable now, so have a good cry together. I don't think crying does any harm to the heart. It may even help to mend it. In any event, just be yourself so long as it includes a little empathy and gentleness. This is not the time to lay a guilt trip on the survivor. Forget the "I told you so", and the lecture about smoking too much or drinking all the time. Nor is this the time for that old line, "What am I going to do now?" That is a good one to talk about with your friend, but not the survivor.

Most people who get to the hospital alive survive and are back home a week or two following their 'coronary event.'[1] They are alive in the physical sense, but often a total wreck on the psychological level. This is especially the case with younger people. A heart attack is not something one expects to experience at a young age. Most middle-aged men, at one time or another, think of having a heart attack but quickly push the scary thought out of their minds by concluding, "Ah it won't happen to me." I venture a guess that

---

1. Coronary event is a cute way of saying heart attack. Many people prefer such euphemisms because heart attack sounds so rough. A more technical term is myocardial infarction. I prefer to simply call a heart attack a heart attack.

most middle-aged women don't even think about it, even though coronary disease is under diagnosed and under treated in women. So when it happens, and you survive, it is a gigantic shock. It is very frightening because it brings you face to face with death, and most western cultures don't prepare people to face death at any age, let alone a young age. The survivors are left with the monumental challenge of trying to put their lives back on track. Too many of these people, both young and old, remain victims for the rest of their lives. They never shake off the victim role. They view themselves as patients, or more precisely victims, and continually look to the medical profession for solutions to what are actually problems in living. Hopefully, your friend or partner will join another group called the Cardiac Champs. Cardiac Champs know a challenge when they see one, but they also meet it. They need some help, but with a little time and support they find a way to enjoy life. This book is a helpful guide for survivors travelling the road from victim to champion. So pass it on to your loved one while he or she is still in the hospital. There is room for one more champion in our club.

**The Cardiac Champ
Does Not
Leave The Hospital A Victim**

II
Wake Up Champ..........You Aren't Dead

Can you believe it? A bloody heart attack. This is scary! I'm on the brink of death. Just like that.......Bang! I'm dead. The kids, work, my car........what happens to everything? This is the pits.

Help! I'm Dying

You got that right! This is no picnic, but let me give you some good news. Twenty-five years ago I was right where you are now. Yup, I was lying in a hospital bed trying to survive my second heart attack in less than three years. In fact, I had just come back from the dead having been revived from a cardiac arrest. I haven't been near a hospital since that time. I have no unreasonable pain, work hard, swim two kilometres alternate days, and take no medications apart from one aspirin every Monday morning and the occasional sedative to help me sleep. In a nutshell, I lead a healthy, vigorous, happy life. So my friend, no doubt at this moment the future looks pretty bleak to you. That is normal. It is hard to think positively while you are stretched out on your back in a hospital bed, but give it a few days. The mood will change. You are still in charge. The big question mark is no longer your survival, but the kind of survivor you want to be. If you are like most heart attack survivors, you probably arrived at the hospital conscious. This means you saw most of the action and remember it. No doubt, you also remember the heart attack. You may have experienced only marginal discomfort or excruciating pain.[2] Regardless, be positive. Just think, you have the makings for a terrific story. If you are an extrovert who wants to dazzle people, you can tell everyone the pain was out of this world.

2. I can share this fabulous insight since I have had the pleasure of both. My first heart attack made me feel like there was a CAT bulldozer on my chest. The second one was a real pussy cat. There was no chest pain, just mild back pain and some unsettling feelings in my upper abdomen.

If you are a woman, tell them it was worse than breach birth with no pain killers. If you are a man, you don't need any lessons from me on how to moan. If you are the quiet type, just say it wasn't that bad. However, introvert or extrovert, there is one point you must remember: whatever your memories, they are of the past. So don't spend a lot of time dwelling on them. That can turn you into a nervous wreck. Focus on the present. For instance, isn't it a weird feeling to find yourself in a hospital bed? It seems like everything has changed so fast....even your night garb. I'd like to punch-out the sonofabitch who invented those hospital gowns. It must have been some pervert with a bum fetish. But if you think the clothing sucks, just wait until you taste the food.

> **The Past Is Gone**
> **The Future Is Still To Come**
> **Just Think Now**

You probably landed in the hospital through the emergency department. If you are like most people, you didn't do a lot of deep thinking in emergency. The negative thoughts usually come a little later. The ol' ticker kept pumping so they moved you into the intensive care unit. That is a good sign because they wouldn't move you if they figured you were going to die. It is much easier to get you to the morgue from emergency than some intensive care unit on the fourth or fifth floor. I won't say much about the ICU because it is just a lie down and do nothing place. Besides, you probably didn't get this book until you were out of there. In most hospitals, after ICU you are moved to a regular coronary ward where you will likely spend five to ten days before going home. The medical types see you staying in the hospital only until your physical health is reasonably good. However, that is the smaller challenge. Your head presents the much bigger challenge!

The Road To Recovery
Runs Through Your Head
Not Your Heart

If you keep reading this book, you will soon discover that your thoughts largely determine how you end up feeling. What we have here is a very simple concept. If you think sad things, you will start feeling sad. Think the worst and you will get depressed real fast. So start being more careful about what thoughts you allow to linger in your noggin. For instance, stop thinking you are going to die any moment. That thought is not a confidence builder. Think upbeat!

The hospital is probably a bigger danger to your health than your cardiac problem, so most of your time there is best spent preparing to leave. It won't take you long to discover that hospitals don't necessarily function in ways that best suit your needs. They are designed more for the convenience of those who work in them. That means the rules and procedures are generally made by people who have never had the pleasure of being a patient in a hospital. [3] The menu designers are a good example. I can't believe they dine in the hospital's cafeteria. I think hospital food is used to keep the patients' stay at a minimum. So let the body heal and get out of there. It is only a week or so out of your life, so play by the rules, but don't spend your entire time sitting around waiting for your body to mend. Start moving around as soon as the nurses give you the green light. The moving about will keep the body well lubricated so you will be able to walk out on your own steam right on schedule. This is also a good time to start working on your head. Begin by taking

---

3. Surely you don't believe it was a pregnant woman who invented stirrups to help the birthing process.

some time to think about the two A's.......acceptance and assurance. I want to say a bit more about these two important traits.

Just A Heart Attack, Mate

A heart attack is like birth. It is painful and starts you out on a new life. You will never be the same. That doesn't mean you are going to be better or worse off. You are simply going to be very different from the way you were before your heart attack. Heart attacks can kill you. So they have an impact. At the very least they bring you face to face with your own mortality. "Hey, wait a minute!" you say. "Death is for very old people, and people who drink and drive. They don't kill the young." Sorry pal, the truth is heart attacks kill people of all ages. But, do you know what? None of that matters now. Whether you are young, middle-aged or an old timer, it is time for you to recognize that you have heart disease. Don't avoid this one. You can't become a Cardiac Champ if you can't accept that you have had a heart attack. The time to deal with this reality is now. You have survived a heart attack. Good! Now face reality and accept that you will have to make some real changes in your life if your survival is to extend beyond a few months.

Any coronary event is a signal that you have not been behaving in healthy ways. This means making some lifestyle changes if you want to reduce the risk. When I speak of lifestyle changes, I am not referring only to such things as your eating, drinking, smoking and exercise habits. I also include the way you relate to people, the thinking methods you use, and how you handle your emotions. It is difficult to change the way you think, feel and act, but change you must if you are to survive much longer. It is your lifestyle that got you where you are, so you had better accept that changes are in order. And the changes have to be ongoing. I caution you against taking the New Year's Eve approach to change. This is where you make all sorts of lifestyle resolutions while you are in a state of fear. All the resolutions you make about clean living while lying in the ICU don't amount to much. Such panic pledges may suit the New Year's Eve scene, but they don't help prevent heart attacks.

Task number one is accepting deep inside the reality that you have had a genuine heart attack. You have to feel this reality inside your guts. You can meet this challenge in a number of ways. You may seek a few quiet moments with your spouse or good friend. Or maybe you want to tell a stranger first. Maybe it is best for you to just quietly repeat to yourself, "I have had a heart attack," a few times. Or you can write lines. I heard of one man who wrote, "I had a very bad heart attack, but I'm alive," two hundred times then handed his lines over to the nurse. He was probably a school teacher. Then there was the artist who worked on acceptance by painting posters that outlined the blockages in her arteries. We all have our own ways for coming to grips with this harsh reality. Just make sure you do it.

It is not simply a matter of giving lip service to the heart attack. "Ya, I had a heart attack. No big deal. Just a bit of bad luck. I'll cut down on the smoking. That's probably what did me in." This is not acceptance. It is rationalization. You must put some energy into understanding and coming to terms with your new reality. A good starting point is to find caring, optimistic people to talk with you. Your spouse, a good friend, or a sympathetic nurse will fill the bill. Most nurses have cared for a lot of cardiacs and watched most of them survive. So they are good people to talk to when trying to accept what has happened to you. The nurses are the best caregivers because they are sophisticated in their medical knowledge and the best in the medical system when it comes to psychology. A physician will pop in and out to check your vitals, ask if you are doing okay, and give a vague answer to any questions of ultimate survival you may pose to him or her. But a nurse? Most are still true Nightingales. Mind you, there are exceptions. Let me tell you a funny story about a nurse I met while in the hospital after my first heart attack. Unfortunately, my initial experience with acceptance was rather harsh. I met a brute of a nurse early my first morning on the coronary ward. I was still quite groggy when she arrived at the side of my bed and shouted,

"Do you know your name?"

"Yes," I replied.

"What is it?" she demanded.

"Larry McConnell," I answered.

"Do you know why you are here?" she snapped back.

Before I had a chance to speak she yelled,

"You had a heart attack. Do you hear me? A heart attack!"

I smiled and she left the room.

This woman was no morale booster. Thankfully, I never saw her again. In retrospect, I guess I fell victim to an over-enthusiastic graduate of some nursing program that emphasized the importance of making sure patients don't deny their condition. I agree; it is bad for you to think you have cancer when you actually have heart disease. However, the orientation program can be gentle and filled with plenty of support. So let me put it to you softly.

Get Real . . .
You Had A Heart Attack!

I don't want to make too big a deal out of this acceptance thing even though most medical staff (who are weird anyway) and psychologists (who are even weirder) find it to be the starting point for recovery. Mind you, the denial process can be played out to the extreme. I witnessed a pretty bizarre scene the second time I was in the intensive care unit. One of the patients got quite upset because the nurse wouldn't let him smoke a cigarette in the ICU. That's denial! I never did get to meet the guy. They probably carried him out in a box! That sort of denial won't do you any good. So give your head a shake. The faster you genuinely accept this setback, the faster you will get on the comeback trail. To help the process along, let's take a look at the other A trait: assurance.

Tell Me I'm Okay

A cardiac survivor needs reassurance more than anything else during the early stages of recovery. A little reassurance breeds hope which is the root of the fighting spirit. I remember well the initial terror that struck me when the physician confirmed that I had had a heart attack. It is quite different from being told that you have a bad case of the flu or a broken leg. It is not even like being told you have an ulcer.[4] A heart attack puts you in the big leagues. Now you really know that fatal moment can strike at any time. Given these scary facts, it is not hard to understand why it takes a bit of practice to become an optimist. You need reassurance so seek it out. Many people first turn to their physician for reassurance. They bombard him or her with questions and requests for information.

- Am I going to live?
- What's the matter with me?
- Am I going to be an invalid?
- How much pain must I endure?
- Do I need an operation?
- Why am I having all these tests?
- How long am I going to be in here?
- When will I know how I am doing?

The questions can go on forever, but there is one question we all want answered more than any other, "Am I going to live?" The

---

4. The ulcer comes a few years later after endless worry about having another heart attack.

quick answer is, "Who knows?" You may be searching for a glimmer of hope here, but in this setting vague responses are the order of the day. The physician will give answers like, "You seem to be doing OK," or "All your vital signs are OK," or "We're waiting for the results of a few tests." Such tentative answers may crank up your anxiety levels, but keep a perspective. The fact is, immediately following a heart attack, no one is in a position to predict where you are going to be in a week or ten days. There are no sure bets, so the best one can do is give you some odds. Are you really up to hearing the odds at this point? Do you really want the medical soothsayer to come along and say, "You know, since you have survived the first twenty-four hours, two weeks, one month, or whatever, the stats show there is a 90/10 or 60/40 or 70/30 chance for survival." Pick any odds you wish. The effect on you will be the same......increased worry.

> ## So Long As You Act Alive
> ## You Will Stay Alive

It is unrealistic to expect the physician to be your fountain of optimism. Most medical practitioners view the body and the spirit as separate entities. Their primary concern is not your psychological well-being. They are trained to deal with illnesses of the body, not the psyche. Most have been taught to understand the functioning of the human body, not the human being. Therefore, most physicians are inclined to view a heart attack as strictly a physical event. Mind you, it certainly is a physical event. Most times the pain makes sure you get that message. However, the impact is not limited to your physical well being. In fact, as time moves along, it becomes more and more evident that the major struggle during recovery is psychological rather than physical.

I am afraid there is not an abundance of outside resources to help you develop a strong sense of hope. The best source is inner strength, but lean a little bit on your loved ones. You should also follow the program set out in this book. Begin by preparing yourself at the mental level. It is important for you to start learning to control your thoughts. Your recovery is going to depend on your becoming much more aware of your thoughts. Do a lot of positive thinking. Positive thoughts manufacture hope.

I am sure it sounds a little peculiar when you are encouraged to start paying attention to your own thoughts. No doubt you are used to simply thinking about whatever comes into your mind. At first it will feel strange examining what you are thinking about, but it is very important for you to do so because your thoughts play a big part in determining how you feel. If you think negatively, you will feel lousy. Think the worst about your health, and you will worry a lot. Think your recovery is hopeless, and you will feel down. This is why it is so important for you to start taking charge of your thinking right after the heart attack when you are suffering with so many discouraging thoughts. The challenge for survivors is to move to the point where they are not continually submerged in pessimistic thinking about their health.

I Think. . .
Therefore I Feel

Angry thoughts and worry thoughts spend a lot of time in the minds of cardiac survivors. The future looks pretty bleak for anyone who remains stuck with their anger over being cursed with a heart attack. Similarly, a life sentence of worry about "When I am going to take the Big One?" doesn't sound very appealing. Those anger and worry thoughts won't do you much good. So, while you're still in the hospital, it is a good idea to start confronting them. Later on in this book I devote a whole section to these destructive thought patterns. In the meantime, you may wish to get started by monitoring your angry and worry thoughts. Nothing very elaborate at this point. You just need to get a better sense of how often you have angry or worry thoughts.

III
From Victim to Champion

In no time flat you will be discharged from the hospital. Discharged....that is a good choice of words because leaving the hospital is a lot like leaving the army. At last you will be able to make some decisions. Imagine, no more asking to go to the bathroom. And best of all, you can start eating real food again. Nothing tops being at home. During the five or ten days you were locked up nothing much will have changed in the world apart from in your little corner of it. You are now a cardiac survivor. No doubt this little jolt has left you worrying about your family, friends and job. I am sure it has also left you feeling a little tentative about the future. It is normal to be worried about these things. What do I tell my loved ones? What about work, my finances, sex, diet? There seem to be a million unanswered questions. Well, slow down. Yes, the cardiac survivor faces a number of changes, but there is no need for events to overwhelm you. You can still be in control of your life.

No question about it, coming home from the hospital after a heart attack is slightly different from returning home after hip surgery or following the removal of your cataracts. Both times I was in hospital, I spent most of my stay thinking about when I was going to die. My confidence didn't get much of a boost from the people who came to visit me, especially my close buddies. They were always uptight because they stood at the end of the bed thinking, "Jesus that could be me lying there." "Come on chum, don't die on me now!" was what one pal said when he arrived to visit, and I happened to be lying in bed with my eyes shut. I was actually surprised when I lasted long enough to leave the hospital. So were most of my buddies! Of course, I was thrilled to be checking out of that medical hotel, but I was not prepared for what lay in store for me. I did not find the transition easy, although it was better the second time. Now, that doesn't mean you should take another heart attack just to improve your transition skills.

I find that heart attack survivors tend to fall into one of two broad categories during recovery. First, there are the 'gorfs' who never really take charge of their lives. They rely heavily on health service providers and are usually depressed for extended periods of time. They feel everything is in the hands of fate. Most of their time is spent waiting for their next heart attack. The second category includes the survivors who accept their setbacks, then take charge of their lives. They know they face some challenges, but they show a determination that leads them to make a few meaningful adjustments while still enjoying life. They usually have a sense of humour, and always a sense of optimism. They lean on their loved ones for help, but also exhibit healthy doses of self-reliance. They are the fighters......the Cardiac Champs! I started out in the gorf mode, so first I will give you a bit of a flavour for that stage of my life.

**The Odds Are Good That
Someday You Will Die Of A
Heart Attack
Now How Do You Plan To Live
In The Meantime**

The Helpless Gorf

Unfortunately, all too many choose the gorf route. It is easy to recognize gorfs. They are instant experts at playing the role of victim. They want, and expect, their spouses to cater to their every whim. Gorfs don't walk about the house; they shuffle along, usually accompanied by significant moaning. I call it the patient shuffle. However, they don't shuffle for long because most of their time is spent sitting on their butts waiting for a bolt of lightning to announce their recovery. It doesn't work. Sitting around doing nothing poses a greater risk than gradually building up your energy levels with activity.

After my first heart attack, I returned home from the hospital under a cloud of doom and gloom. I was the helpless gorf who had been struck down by the BIG ONE. That was my first experience with a serious illness, and let me assure you I did not leave the hospital feeling confident and eager about getting back on track. I was scared. Actually, that is understating it. I was terrified! Mind you, hospitals tend to breed dependence. Think about it. Most of your time is spent in your pyjamas, lying on your back in bed, while you are catered to, or tolerated, by nurses. If the truth be known, most hospitals are depressing places that favour submissive, dependent types who sleep a lot and don't wet the bed. I didn't sleep much, struggled with the submissive bit, but never wet the bed. It was ten days of loneliness that sapped most of my fighting spirit from me.

Like most people, I left the hospital in the victim mode. I was a helpless gorf who was afraid to move a limb. I must say, my confidence wasn't helped when the nurse insisted I be taken to the front door in a wheelchair. She claimed that was just a precaution for insurance purposes. I guess the hospital would have been liable if I had had a heart attack dancing with my wife in the elevator. In any event, I left the hospital a shaken man. I moved about with extreme caution believing the slightest degree of exertion would produce another heart attack. I was already entrenched in the sick guy role before leaving the hospital, and I continued to play it when I got home. I remember the scene well.

My wife and brother-in-law had picked me up at the hospital and driven me home. When we arrived, I insisted that my brother-in-law carry me upstairs on his back claiming I wasn't ready to climb stairs. He struggled up the ten stairs with me hanging over his shoulders. This weight-lifting chore probably put him at risk for a heart attack! Besides, now I realize that hanging onto his back took more energy than walking up the stairs, but it was a pretty impressive show. He finally managed to carry me up to my bedroom and drop me onto the bed. The good thing was being back in my own home. The weird thing was going straight to bed. Folks, this is not the way to do it. Straight to your own bed from the hospital bed won't do you much good.

Eventually, ever so slowly, I started to fight the victim role. I began to realize that I couldn't just sit around waiting for the Big One. I took a careful look at myself and decided to make some changes. Unfortunately, my initial efforts didn't help much. I followed the New Year's Eve route and made a bunch of resolutions. I got real intense about quitting smoking, doing regular exercise, and following a good diet. I gave up smoking soon after the attack, completely changed my diet to a bland nonfat one, and exercised like an athlete. I was just following the doctor's orders......eat well, exercise and don't smoke. It never occurred to me that a heart attack was anything other than a physical sickness, and I was a psychologist! I never thought about or analyzed things like anger, relationships, or being extremely uptight. I didn't realize these psychological matters were related to the functioning of my heart. My focus on the purely physical seemed fairly reasonable at the time, but it wasn't enough. I was back in the hospital in less than three years. The second time around I took a more comprehensive approach that included my psychological and social life. More of that later.

Hey Champ

Cardiac Champs are easy to define. They are survivors who manage to live a happy, meaningful life even though they have experienced a heart attack, heart surgery, or some other serious cardiovascular problem. Cardiac Champs feel in control without denying that their medical history has been scary at times. The budding Cardiac Champ arrives home eager to resume a regular routine in quick order. This includes being out of bed, three square meals, a little exercise, visits from friends, lots of laughs, and contemplating goals for the future. The Cardiac Champ recognizes the pitfalls of the victim role so sets out on an active course from the start. A gorf puts the focus on limitations while a champ concentrates on potential.

> **One Good Way To Avoid Being Sick Is To Avoid Acting Sick**

Cardiac Champs' levels of activity increase rather quickly because they have no desire to remain a patient for very long. Once home, they avoid remaining in pyjamas twenty-four hours a day. In the morning they get up, get washed and dressed, and take the time to notice and appreciate the progress they are making from day to day. They also recognize the importance of starting to walk about their house. If they live in a house with stairs, they aren't afraid to walk down a stair or two and back up a stair or two. Slowly at first, but deliberately. Of course, within as short a period of time as possible, they are walking outside. In the meantime, they open their windows to make sure they breathe fresh air and get a look at their familiar neighbourhood. In other words, successful recuperation requires you to avoid acting like an invalid where progress is at such a slow pace you piss everybody off around you by becoming a general pain in the ass. This doesn't mean that you should go it alone. It just means that support and help are a lot easier to give to someone with an upbeat attitude. So perk up, and set a plan of care in motion that will get you beyond the hospital's support services. The road to being a Cardiac Champ is a bumpy one, but it is certainly not beyond your reach. It takes some work, and it takes some change, but the results are worth it. The remainder of this book is devoted to helping you become a Cardiac Champ. Go get 'em champ!

IV
Reaching Out

Most cardiac survivors need emotional support both while they are in the hospital, and when they return home. The problem is where to find it. In most hospitals, the cardiac patient is cared for by a team of health care professionals. In the smaller hospitals the team will usually be limited to a physician and a couple of nurses while the large urban hospitals usually have a larger team that includes nurses, dieticians, surgeons, physiotherapists, cardiologists and general practitioners. The composition of these professional teams clearly reflects the medical world's belief that heart attacks are essentially physical events. These helpers are highly trained specialists who know a lot about bodies, but not much about the psychological needs of survivors. They define the causal factors strictly in physical terms so it stands to reason that their treatment will be directed at your body. Indeed, there is no popular medical model that calls for vigorous treatment of the psychological aspects of heart disease.

The old adage that a healthy mind makes for a healthy body holds marginal status in the actual practice of medicine. Most medical teams will be represented by a number of disciplines but rarely, if ever, is counselling psychology one of them. A visit from a social worker or a minister while in hospital is likely to be the only visible acknowledgement of your psychological being. The medical system is designed to fix up your body, not develop peace of mind. As a result, the helping professionals devote their energies to encouraging the cardiac survivor to stop smoking, exercise, eat healthy foods, and take medications as prescribed by the physician. The worry, stress and anger that inevitably accompany heart disease are not deemed a priority by medical professionals. The connection between the state of your mind and the health of your heart somehow gets lost in the shuffle. Unfortunately, I never realized the significance of this gap in services until months after my second heart attack.

I recovered from my first heart attack in a medium-sized Canadian hospital that provided excellent physical care, but no psychological assistance. Once I left the hospital, a public health nurse visited my home on two or three occasions to take my blood pressure, ensure I was walking each day, and give me advice about my diet. That was it. I returned to the hospital a month later for an angiogram. The test confirmed an irregularity in my right coronary artery near the posterior descending vessel, and a blockage in my left coronary artery beyond the first diagonal. The physician who gave me this cheery news was a sincere, caring person, but had no training in psychological counselling. I was a wreck with a new worry....... confirmed clogged arteries! Actually, this was not a world-shattering diagnosis for it only suggested the early onset of atherosclerosis, but I immediately envisioned myself dying during by-pass surgery. The best the physician could offer was the suggestion that I take Ativan for my nerves. I had never taken pills for anxiety before, and I was too afraid to start.[5]

Apart from a few routine checkups, I had little to do with medical practitioners for the two years plus between my heart attacks. However, after my second episode I reached out in desperation and latched onto a formal rehabilitation program. I had taken the heart attack and gone into cardiac arrest while on vacation in British Columbia.[6] Actually a lot of people take heart attacks on their vacations. It is probably because we uptight folks can't handle the

---

5. This was actually good advice, but I didn't follow it until after my second heart attack a couple of years later.

6. This may have been an episode of coronary insufficiency related to coronary spasm. I never did get a clear diagnosis or an explanation for the unstable angina and cardiac arrest.

relaxation. Anyway, upon returning to my home in Edmonton, I saw a cardiologist who strongly recommended that I attend the cardiac rehabilitation program that was offered out of the hospital. At this point in my victim career I was ready to try anything, so I signed up.

My group of cardiac survivors included a dozen people of various ages all with distinct personalities and unique struggles. There were a couple of gentle women who looked to be in their seventies and five or six men in their fifties. Another guy who looked almost fifty was recovering from by-pass surgery, and the one young fellow in the group seemed to be in total denial. Then there was me........the mad guy. It sure was a collection of very different people, but we all had at least one common need........support. Our group leader was a nurse who acted like a displaced drill sergeant. I don't know what kind of a nurse she was, but I presume she had some training in coronary care.

The first session was devoted to testing the dirty dozen. They checked our hearts, measured our blood pressure, and had us take a walk on a treadmill. This all took place in some kind of exercise room. The best was still to come. Once we were done with the treadmill, the nurse announced that we were all going to the x-ray department. We were issued a hospital gown. The nurse told us to strip to the waist, put on the hospital gown and follow her down the hallway to the x-ray department. Once there, we waited in a corridor until the technician called our number. She didn't talk....just pointed a lot. It gave you that military school feeling. Let me assure you I was not a happy camper, before, during or after this session. Nevertheless, I persisted and showed up for the next one.

The second session was a lot more inspiring than the first one. The victims sat in chairs facing the nurse who got quite excited while telling us all about heart attacks and how to prevent the next one. A real scary lecture. I particularly remember her graphic descriptions about the horrors of advanced angina. She told us there were a couple of men on the coronary ward who had to be hospitalized because their angina was so bad. Great news for a guy just getting over a heart attack! I think the scare tactic was designed to have us all instantly quit smoking. I certainly didn't enjoy my cigarette after that session. In fact, it took quite a few beers to calm me down. The third session was a lecture on good nutrition. Eating my porridge every morning may impress the nutritionist, but it is no consolation for having to spend the entire night worrying about whether or not I am going to wake up the next morning. I quit the program.

> # The Cardiac Survivor Craves Empathy Not Recipes

Obviously the very act of joining a rehab group constituted reaching out. But what was I reaching out for? I already knew everyone wanted me to quit smoking, eat healthy food and exercise. Great advice, just at the wrong time. Cardiac survivors can't handle a lot of advice. We want to know if we are going to live. We want to get some confidence. We want to talk. We want to be heard. We need a sympathetic ear and someone prepared to help us grapple with our anger and fear. The idea of a rehabilitation group is a good one, but it must focus on the psychological struggles of recovery. The cardiac survivor needs to talk. We need help with the powerful emotions we experience following a heart attack. The primary struggle after a heart attack takes place in the head. At this point, the spotlight belongs on our feelings, not our diets. There will be plenty of time to discuss the benefits of broccoli and cauliflower. The immediate need is our psychological well-being.

The Happy Helpers

I have met cardiac survivors who are not fortunate enough to be involved in a healthy intimate relationship. That is too bad. Such a relationship can have as much to offer your health as medicine. Actually, we humans are quite needy for mutually supportive, personal relationships, both intimate and less intense ones. Most can use a bit of romance and passion in their life, but we also need good friends who are loyal and supportive in our times of greatest need. It is my good fortune to have a happy, romantic relationship that has been going strong for over forty years. I also have two adult sons who are fantastic people. My life is further enriched by several close friends including some who went to elementary school with me. These kinds of relationships take on special meaning when your life bumps into tragedy. These are the people who will accompany you on the road to recovery. Be good to them.

Love.....An Itching In The Heart That Unclogs Arteries

The road to recovery is generally a lot smoother when you travel it with someone else. You need the help of other people. However, the lecture-type group I experienced will leave most cold. The most helpful caregiver is the spouse, friend, or professional who can help you express and cope with the fear of dying, who can help you deal with that pissed off feeling for being in this mess, and who can help you figure out some way to stop worrying. So shop around. Perhaps it is best to look beyond the hospital. One option is to contact the local Heart and Stroke Foundation. The public health system is another referral source you may want to contact for assistance. This organization will be familiar with the services in your community. It is also a good resource for finding the location of any self-help groups in your area. A self-help group can offer tremendous support because it brings you into contact with other people who know what it is like to survive a heart attack. In such a group you will also meet people who have already put their lives back together. Exposure to these Cardiac Champs is bound to have a positive influence on your recovery. Seeking professional counselling is also an option, but it is usually very expensive for most people. Finally, don't forget that family and friends can offer great support.

If you are married, it is virtually guaranteed that your heart attack will have a long lasting impact on your marital relationship. However, the impact need not be a negative one. I think if your marriage was wretched before the heart attack, it will probably be wretched after it. Similarly, a happy marriage can survive a heart attack. However, even when the marital relationship is idyllic, a heart attack is extremely disruptive to the family's life. It is not only the cardiac survivor who is under stress. Everyone waiting at home is under a great deal of strain while you are in the hospital. A heart attack creates a great deal of uncertainty about the immediate future. Family members start to sense that things will have to be different around the house. They now have someone with heart disease in the family, so they presume some changes are in order, but what kind of changes?

The spouse is definitely the forgotten one in the treatment of cardiac survivors. It is amazing, but true, that most caregivers presume the only person requiring help is the heart attack survivor. This assumption is a mistake. Remember, it was only a couple of weeks ago that your partner was rolling along thinking all was more or less right with the world. Then your heart attack or a stroke or open heart surgery! Things change fast. Now your partner must care for you, look after the kids, run the household, and go to work while keeping an upbeat attitude so that you won't worry about anything. That is a lot of pressure that can produce plenty of mixed emotions.

It is easy to feel a lot of bitterness and anger toward the cardiac survivor. I don't want to overwhelm you,[7] but you should appreciate that heart attacks are a big pain in the ass for the innocent bystander. So, ever so delicately, I would like to suggest that it would be real smart for you to muster up your courage and consider not only your own needs, but those of the ones around you. It is important to remember that the change process primarily belongs to you, not your spouse. And here I talk of positive change. You must be the first to come to grips with your worry, anger, poor eating habits, stationary lifestyle, and smoking if that is part of your repertoire. You had the heart attack, not your spouse. And remember, your family members will be a little uptight as they begin to sort out the ramifications of this life event. So take a look around and see how you can help.

> **Get It Straight...**
> **You Don't Have Heart Disease**
> **You Are Arterially Challenged**

Many cardiac survivors find it difficult to focus on dynamics that have no direct impact on their needs. Once home from the hospital, they tend to be very egocentric, impatient, and demanding in their personal relationships. They are not pressed to use their listening skills as conversation tends to focus on their own medical trials and tribulations. Not surprisingly, they quickly adjust to all the pampering they receive from their mates. With couples the ordeal, in some ways, is more taxing for the partner. It is a frightening experience that conjures up some very powerful emotions that must be kept in check while he or she maintains the household and visits the cardiac survivor in the hospital. Imagine the horror they experience while

---

7. I can't overburden you here, because I expect you to die from heart failure not guilt.

standing guard on the home front when you are teetering on the brink of death. Terror reigns that first night while they wait at home alone wondering if they are going to be single come morning. This has to be a very scary time. The first few days can be overwhelming for any spouse who must grapple with the very real possibility that his or her partner might die. Survivors must also remember that while they are in the hospital, all the resources tend to be mobilized around them. Few people think of their partners' needs.

It is worth remembering that often the passport to healthy living is helping other people. Helping others is good therapy for a cardiac survivor because the helping process generally benefits both the person seeking help and the person giving help. You are not the only one worried about the future. The struggle is equally painful for your mate who must come to grips with the same issue, just from a different perspective. Probably the question on everyone's mind is, "How long are you going to be around?" No one can answer that question, but it is important to recognize that in a family system, the fallout from heart attacks hits beyond the survivor. It can be therapeutic to give others the chance to share this fright. I strongly recommend that you have a go at the helper role.

> ### Helping Other People Is
> ### Good For Everyone's Heart

If you have children, consider that a parent's heart attack can be as traumatic, or more so, for the children as it is for the spouse or the survivor. It may create significant adjustment problems for the children as they attempt to understand and cope with the apparent tentativeness of their parent's cardiac condition. In fact, it is not uncommon for children to experience intense levels of anxiety once they discover why you are in the hospital. The anxiety reactions are even more debilitating for your children if you are a single parent.

The decision of when and how to tell the children warrants careful attention. Unfortunately, it is a decision the spouse must usually make alone while you are in the hospital. Once the survivor arrives home, the primary task is to build up the youngsters' confidence by reassuring them that you are on the mend. This is no time to be a moaner. Your role as a parent is to provide emotional support to your children, not seek it from them. Therefore, even if you are a born pessimist, it is crucial for you to present as a positive, optimistic person. It is your responsibility to help your children cope with this trauma whenever you decide to tell them. This is a matter that should not be taken lightly, for a parent's heart attack can have serious ramifications on the psychological health of the children. You must deal very sensitively with the insecurity and uncertainty that is bound to haunt your children. It may even be a good idea to enlist the assistance of a school counsellor or favourite aunt so the children will have the opportunity to express their fears with someone they trust other than the parent. This can be useful because many youngsters will hesitate to express their true feelings to the parent out of fear that their upset, if shown, will be bad for the cardiac's health.

My children were very young when I took my heart attacks. I had a newborn and a two year old when I took the first one They visited me in the hospital, but we simply told the two year old that I was getting my back fixed. They were three and five at the time of my second heart attack. At this point, the older son was aware that our normal routines were temporarily interrupted, but we did not provide him with all of the gory details. This meant I had plenty of time to prepare for telling them. In fact, I waited until each of them reached the age of twelve before I told them of my medical history. Of course, the option 'to tell or not to tell' does not exist with older children. A parent can't spend a week or ten days in the hospital with their teenage children believing they are simply in for a little rest because a Caribbean cruise was too expensive.

Hey You! Out Of The Closet

I have discovered a rather intriguing phenomenon over the years. There are many cardiac survivors with a strong desire to keep their heart disease a secret. They think, apart from family and a few close friends, the fewer who know about their condition the better. This urge to keep the Big One a dark secret is sometimes connected to work. Some survivors fear being treated as weak people where their perceived physical limitations are unfairly taken into consideration when making decisions in the workplace. Superiors may view coronary problems as a real handicap so may be reluctant to advance survivors in their employment. However, I believe a much more dominant reason, particularly with men, is their fear of being perceived as weak or unable to handle pressure, especially in their places of employment. There is a lot of popular literature out there today that links the early onset of coronary disease to stress. Who wants to be perceived as a guy who can't handle stress? Not very macho! Those who reason this way opt to keep their medical history a secret. This sort of paranoia won't cause you much harm so long as you have come to grips with the reality of your heart attack, and have some confidantes around for comfort in your times of emotional trauma.

I was one of those cardiac survivors who wanted as few people as possible to know of my plight. Of course, this kind of undercover mission is hard to pull off unless a lot of uncontrollable events unfold in your favour. It is hard for most of us to disappear for a couple of months and have no questions asked upon our return. However, after my second heart attack events did unfold in my favour to the point where I was able to live the life of a closet cardiac for a decade. I had my second attack a couple of months before I changed jobs and moved to another city. I couldn't have planned it better. New city, new job, new life. I did not tell my secret to anyone. In fact, I spent the next ten years as the CEO of a large nonprofit organization where the only person aware of my medical history during that time was the one who typed the first draft outline of this manuscript. I lived and worked in that city for over ten years without anyone knowing I had experienced heart attacks. I am not sure why I chose to keep it such a secret, although with this book, I am obviously out of the closet. Nothing extreme about my personality.

Who Me? A Heart Attack? Are You Kidding?

I should tell you, the life of a closet cardiac has its embarrassing moments. There was one I experienced repeatedly every winter for ten years following my cardiac arrest. During that decade I lived in one of Canada's major snow belts. That meant a lot of snow to shovel, and a lot of stuck cars. I couldn't push cars, so it got really awkward in a snowstorm when a neighbour pushed my car out of the driveway, then sought my help with his car. This frequent request forced me to develop a very convincing facial grimace that made it appear as though I was pushing the car with all my strength, when in fact all of my exertion was directed at making the grimace. Obviously, I had a very poor success rate when it came to getting cars out of snow banks. Indeed, I was well known in the neighbourhood as a little guy who tried real hard, but just wasn't very strong. Damn! There's that macho thing again. Nevertheless, on balance I was glad to have had the anonymity for that decade, although the circumstances that allow for such privacy are rare.

V
Return From the Dead

A heart attack brings a lot of uncertainty into the family. All the family members must confront a number of new challenges. Hopefully, if married with children, the well-being of your spouse and children is a top priority, but their progress is very closely linked to your rate of recovery. In other words, their capacities to cope increase as you demonstrate a growing ability to get on with your life. Here I speak particularly of the more mundane aspects of life such as money, sex and work. Your ability to manage these parts of your life effectively sends a strong message of recovery to your loved ones. So what will you face upon your return to work? What about money? And, oh yes, your sex life, is it over? These are important issues that warrant further discussion, so let's take a few moments to consider them.

Okay Boss, I'm Back

The vast majority of us face a very clear reality........no work, no money. So return to work? We must. The ease of your re-entry into the workplace is certainly influenced by the attitude and behaviour of your coworkers and employer. Nevertheless, the amount of satisfaction you gain from your employment is the key factor. If you are reasonably satisfied with your job, you will probably not find your return to work a big deal. Alternatively, if you are unhappy with your work because it threatens your ego, makes you angry, or offers minimal satisfaction, then you may well experience intensified problems upon your return. However, whether you are a happy camper or a job hater, I would suggest you take the time to systematically prepare for your return to work. Your first day back will be a hell of an experience. It may surprise or frustrate you, but many people will treat you differently when you return to work.

some will treat it as a return from the dead. Others will view you as damaged goods so no longer capable. Heart attacks get attention because most people are afraid of them. They can kill! Hey, you survived so now you are a celebrity. It won't last long, but for awhile you can bask in the limelight.

There is no rule for determining when a cardiac survivor should return to work. The sooner the better is probably the best advice for most of us, but many factors must be taken into consideration when making that decision. The degree of damage to the heart muscle, the rate of the healing process, the survivor's confidence level, the available support system, and the type of work are all valid factors to be considered when attempting to establish a time for returning to work. However, it is quite common, barring unusual complications, for cardiac survivors to be back on the job five or six weeks after their heart attack. This can seem like a very long way off for some people, particularly if they have no medical insurance or are self-employed and unable to afford the downtime. Others may find the recuperation period long because they are bored. Whatever the reasons for wanting a quick return to work, my only advice is don't push it. Mind you, not everyone finds the recuperation period too long. Some wish it could last four or five months. This is often the attitude with people who hate their jobs. They want to extend their sick time to the limit. It is also a particularly appealing idea for those who have a generous health plan at work and enjoy just hanging around. Of course, most employers require a medical certificate, so you will need the cooperation of a physician. If you are good at moaning, most physicians will agree to three months if for no other reason than to get rid of you. I am afraid if you want more than three months, you will have to opt for bypass surgery or a heart transplant.

It is probably a good idea to give your supervisor a call a day or two before you return to work. Indicate that you would like to visit the boss the day before you return to work, or first thing in the morning on the day you arrive back on the job. It may surprise you, but the whole business of your returning to work can be quite difficult for an employer. Many feel uncomfortable even raising the most practical issues with you. However, they have a legitimate need to know so you should not hesitate to advise them of the circumstances. The key is to be straightforward with your employer. It is important that they have all the details. Therefore, you should advise them if it will be necessary for you to go for tests and keep physicians' appointments during working hours. Naturally the employer will also be most interested to learn if you are able to return to your normal duties or if you need a gradual transition. If it was deemed necessary for you to return to work on a part-time basis and perform only select functions, then you should up-front this with the employer and do your best to negotiate mutually agreeable arrangements. Likewise, if you are able to fully resume your original job functions, it is important for you to make this clear to the employer.

The reality for most cardiac survivors is that they are not going to move and they are not going to switch jobs. So they will likely be in the spotlight for awhile upon their return to work. You are a bit of a story now. Some people will feel awkward around you. You may even make them a bit nervous because they perceive you as somewhat of a time bomb. You know, "He can drop dead at any moment," or "We don't want to get Sally too riled up or she will end up taking another heart attack." This approach can rile you up. Don't let it. Look on the bright side. There is not much you can do about people's reactions, but you can certainly determine your response to their reactions. You have some real power here. Just act like you are about to croak anytime you aren't getting your own way.

Or take your cue and play the role of the martyr. Exploit it for all it is worth. The options are unlimited, for most of your workmates are unnerved by your brush with death.

Most cardiac survivors prefer to share their feelings with only a chosen few. They really don't want their health to be a topic of conversation in the workplace. However, be prepared for a barrage of questions. They will come from your superiors, subordinates, those who know you best at work, and even some of your casual acquaintances. This probing can be stressful, so prepare for the onslaught before you return to work. The response will differ depending on whether you are being questioned by a boss or workmate. Nevertheless, expect such encounters and develop a general plan for responding to them. You can certainly limit the number of questions and probings by being prepared to offer brief and direct responses.

There is no best way for answering questions about your health. The key is to settle on an approach that leaves you feeling good. Below is an example of a series of polite responses that would let most interrogators know that you wish to avoid a prolonged conversation about the state of your health.

Inquisitor:	How are you doing?
Cardiac Champ:	Well, thanks.
Inquisitor:	I'll tell ya, you sure had quite a setback.
Cardiac Champ:	Ya I had a heart attack, but they tell me it was fairly routine so I was only in the hospital a week. Then I rested a while at home.
Inquisitor:	It must have been pretty tough in the hospital.
Cardiac Champ:	Not really. Apart from lying around for the first couple of days, nothing very eventful happened to me. Got a few tests, saw a dietician, rested in bed a few days, then they sent me home.

Of course, the questions can persist and become somewhat unsettling for the cardiac survivor. However, you can escape by simply saying that you have to move along. Tell them you have a doctor's appointment.

I should mention there are a few cardiac survivors who thrive on reliving all their hospital experiences with their workmates. They find it therapeutic to tell about their time in emergency, intensive care and recuperating at home to anyone who will listen to every detail. Personally, I think such motor mouths just like to be morbid. They sense the listener is uptight so they give out all the gruesome details. However, if it works for you, ramble on until the listener gets bored or simply goes away.

The need to respond to your colleagues' and superiors' questions regarding the state of your arteries is not the major challenge you face upon your return to work. It is you. Most cardiac survivors approach their work with a significant amount of competitiveness, intensity and, in many instances, overt hostility. These powerful emotions rarely work in your best interest. Their presence explains why the workplace is the primary source of stress for so many people. There are all kinds of reasons for experiencing tension at work but none of them helps us to maintain a healthy heart. Many people are locked into jobs they wish to leave. Others like the work, but hate the boss or other colleagues. You may have no control over the conditions or people who get you uptight or angry, but that doesn't mean you can't change your responses. You must begin to recognize that you, rather than the person you are reacting to, control your emotions. It is you who decides whether or not to become angry at the boss or worry about month end sales reports. You have just had a heart attack. It is time to chill out. The mental strain associated with intense emotional responses is generally destructive. You must find a new way to cope with the stress of the ordinary workday. The key question is how do you do this?

The emphasis on changing your environment has to shift to learning how to cope with your environment. The chances are pretty good that prior to your heart attack you had a tendency to approach people at work as either enemies or friends. We cooperate with friends and screw enemies. Great attitude, but it needs a slight revision if the workplace is not to hinder your health. Attitude change? Ya, it sounds awful, but it is time to ease up and recognize that some things are just going to be this way because that is the way they are. This does not mean you must lie down and play dead, although that will come sooner than you think if you persist in trying to fight the unbeatable battle. You don't have to be a wimp, but you have to learn to handle situations without allowing frustration to build up to a point where anger is your most commonly felt emotion. Therefore, it is important for you to change the friend/enemy dichotomy to friends and colleagues. Friends are the people that you like, that you want to be with after work, that you enjoy spending time with during work, and like to have on your team. Colleagues are the rest of the people who are present in your work life. You may have no control over how your colleagues behave, but you do have full control over how you react to them.

> ### Indifference Is A Tremendous Substitute For Anger

The urge to compete with everybody in sight is also a good characteristic to discard in the workplace. It is time to relax and begin to enjoy both your friends and colleagues at work. This enjoyment can be gained without you being the centre of attention, and certainly there is no need for you to be the loudest one in the group at all times. Too many cardiac survivors are unable to sit back and enjoy the world. They have to be constantly shaping events at work. This is a very demanding approach that grants no one great health if they persist in it at all costs. There is a time and a place to be the leader of the parade, but the maintenance of good health also requires you to occasionally reap the benefits that come from sitting back and watching others succeed at leadership. The aggressive, loud, dominant personality is not an uncommon one with cardiac survivors. Many have a lot of acquaintances, but few friends, a marital relationship with no depth, and an unwillingness to look at their own behaviour. Beating everybody at debate, earning money, and maintaining high productivity may bring you some satisfaction, but not without a steep price. All too often the price is severe anxiety and anger, two psychological responses that frequently dominate the cardiac survivor's response repertoire. They are destructive forces that must be conquered if you are to move from victim to champion. However, more about them later. First, let me say a few words about your money and your sex life.

The Money Machine

It doesn't take most cardiac survivors very long to start worrying about money. If you live in a country where there is no universal medical coverage, you are likely facing a huge medical bill. If your employer doesn't offer paid medical leave, you are also faced with lost income. As well, survivors worry about whether their earning potential will be affected by their newly discovered heart disease. Then there is the cardiac survivor's bottom line question, "What if I die.........Where is my money going to go?" Hopefully, most of it won't go to the tax collector.

There is no standard formula for dealing with these money matters. Much depends on where you live, the kind of job you have and the total value of your assets. I am not a wealthy person, but I have been lucky when it comes to money issues. My earning potential has not been affected by my heart attacks because my work hasn't required physical prowess. I also wasn't faced with overwhelming medical bills when I left the hospital. I am fortunate to live in Canada where there is universal medical insurance.[8] My first heart attack didn't affect my income as I had no job, and with my second one, I worked for an employer that had a generous sick plan. However, the question of what would happen to my money if I died loomed heavily upon me.

Have A Little Cash? A Few Assets? Make Sure You Have A Will!

I made a will. It leaves everything to my wife if I die before her. Likewise if she dies first, everything goes to me. We also appointed a guardian for our children in case we died at the same time before they reached adulthood. You never know, we could have ended up taking fatal heart attacks together.

These kinds of arrangements, particularly if you have children, make sense whether or not you have heart disease. It is one less thing for you to worry about in a crisis. The preparation of a will need not be a very complicated affair for most people. In my case, I got a self-help book and made up my own will. It was later reviewed by a lawyer friend to ensure all was in order. If you have no money or assets, obviously this is no big deal. However for most, having a will makes sense. I am not a financial expert so can offer only limited guidance here. Indeed, unless your financial affairs are very straightforward, I suggest you approach a professional for assistance. Now, let's forget about money matters for awhile and talk about a <u>much more important</u> subject.

8. I travel a lot, but I always make sure I take my heart attacks in a country with a universal health care system.

A Roll In The Hay

Lying alone in bed for eight or ten days is no picnic for a sexually active individual. After the first few days, it strikes like a bolt of lightning....is this it? No more sex? The goddamn heart attack should have killed me. Relax. Most cardiacs have these thoughts while in the hospital. It is a sign that you are getting better. After all, you must be starting to think you're going to live for awhile if you're worrying about your sex life. Shift gears. Let a few erotic thoughts creep into your mind. They will quickly wipe out your pessimistic thinking.

Most cardiac survivors are concerned about their future sex life, but they refrain from discussing their worries with the health providers looking after them. Mind you, on this one follow your instincts because most nurses and physicians are no more knowledgeable about sexual matters than the lay person. In fact, most are just as happy as you are to leave the subject alone. The downside? In all probability, you will leave the hospital none the wiser regarding your future potential for maintaining your status as the greatest love maker of all time. But not to worry.......the chances are excellent that passion will drive you to resume your normal sex life shortly after your return from the hospital.[9] You will not be sentenced to join the sexually challenged.

> **If It Feels Good
> Do It**

I think the best predictor for the quality of your sex life after a heart attack is the quality of your sex life before the heart attack. If you were somewhat of a puritan prior to your heart attack, it

---

9. I have to qualify this by saying I am presuming you are reasonably healthy on the physical front apart from the heart disease. Obviously, if you have a host of other ailments and use multiple medications you could encounter a few sexual problems.

is unlikely that you will turn into a sex-starved maniac upon your return from the hospital. Similarly, if you enjoyed sex regularly with your partner before the coronary, it is unlikely that you will practice celibacy following your heart attack. Nevertheless, it is not unusual for cardiac survivors to be very cautious when they first return from the hospital. You and your partner may be somewhat tentative in your sexual encounters. In fact, at first you may have to fight thoughts such as "If I get too aroused, the excitement will kill me!" Such fear is not uncommon, but you must show a little resistance. Try out a counter thought, "Dangerous arousal? Oh, but what a way to go." Seriously, there are not too many death certificates where the reason for death reads 'sexual play.' Sexual enjoyment is not known as a high risk business. If you can climb a flight or two of stairs, you are probably in good enough shape for a bit of sex.

The cardiac survivor's partner is also bound to experience some anxiety. There is a genuine fear that if you get wildly passionate your cardiac survivor will get out of control and die in a state of erotic madness. Relax. Such worries are generally short-lived if you seek reassurance from your partner. Allow yourself to be tentative, but talk openly about your fears with your partner, and don't forget, for most, sex is not much of an aerobic workout. Mind you, if your partner is an overweight brute who uses sex as an alternative to gymnastics, you may wish to proceed with caution to see if he or she experiences any chest pain. Regardless, the cardiac's body will let him or her know when enough is enough long before the heart is in imminent danger. The wonderful thing about sex is it gives so much enjoyment for so little exertion. That is why there will always be more lovers than joggers!

VI
Who Said Don't Panic?

It is very difficult to stop worrying about your health once you have had a heart attack. Indeed the worry can be overwhelming at times. I know the feeling. I have been a combatant in the worry battle for decades. It even intrudes into my recreational life. I have been swimming at the YMCA three or four times a week for the past twenty-five years. I remember feeling particularly uptight one day while I was on my way to the YMCA. My legs felt limp. There was a knot in my stomach. My head felt spacey, and I started feeling pain in my chest. "Oh shit," I thought, "another uptight, miserable swim!"

I arrived at the 'Y', changed into my bathing suit, and walked to the pool wondering if it was wise for me to go swimming when I felt this way. The chest pain was not a clear-cut pain. It felt more like a tight knot, although it was hard to distinguish it from the tightness I was feeling in my stomach. Mind you, these were not new sensations. I often felt really uptight worrying about whether or not I was about to have another heart attack. I still experience such feelings from time to time, but not nearly as frequently or as intensely as in past years. Nevertheless, such feelings or sensations create a real dilemma for cardiacs. Is this when you are supposed to stop and rest, go to the hospital, go home, or is it just your nerves working overtime? Why all the indecision you may wonder? So what if it is only nerves. The solution seems to be a straightforward one. If you don't feel up to it, just don't do it. Why take any chances? Sounds logical, except the bloody nerves are around an awful lot. So if you continually give into the symptoms, you will end up a shut-in. Then again, if you don't give into the right symptoms, at the right time, you will end up dead. A real Catch-22.

> **If You Give In To All Your Symptoms**
> **They Will Paralyze You**
> **If You Ignore The Crucial Symptoms**
> **They Will Kill You**

I jumped into the pool and started to swim my laps. My body was tight. Real tight. I told myself to keep going slowly, as long as there was no increase in the pain. I tried to combat the physical sensations by concentrating on my breathing. I exhaled forcefully to create a gurgling, rhythmic sound in the water. This helped distract me from the varied sensations running through my body, but it didn't completely shut off my mind.

"That pain does seem to be in my chest," I thought.

"What if these are the early warning signs of a heart attack?"

I persisted for a few more laps. After about six laps I thought,

"It doesn't seem to be getting any worse. My stomach has settled down. My head feels OK."

I continued to swim as my thoughts of fear battled with my emerging sense of confidence. I decided to swim fifteen laps waiting for the symptoms to vanish........so long as they didn't get any worse. The physical symptoms gradually began to disappear one by one. I could feel my body starting to relax in the water. My confidence began to block out the worry, and by the fifteenth lap my mind had turned to other thoughts. I ended up swimming my usual two kilometres.

Worry is a tormenting companion to the cardiac survivor. In fact, at times our imagination and capacity to worry can send us into states of absolute terror. This is anxiety at its worst........the panic attack! I still remember my first panic attack. I was living in Edmonton where

I had started working after recovering from my first heart attack. I was sent to a four-day workshop in Toronto. The first night I went out to dinner with some friends, but returned early to my hotel room. I was feeling restless. I tried listening to the radio, reading the newspaper, looking out the window, reading a book.........nothing seemed to settle me down. I went to bed. Then I started thinking about my heart. When a cardiac survivor starts thinking about his heart, sooner rather than later, he is going to start thinking about heart pain.

In a matter of moments I was on the side of the bed rubbing my chest to ensure there was no pain. There was none; but without warning a terror mechanism went off in my head. I was overwhelmed by the fear of dying on the spot. I just couldn't maintain a perspective. Death seemed a sure thing. I tried to fight it. I was saying aloud, "I've got to hold on here. I don't want to die." I could feel the sweat pouring off me. I got up and turned on the light. I still wasn't feeling any pain, yet I was convinced I was about to die! I still remember hearing voices from the next room and trying to use them as my source of reality. Somehow I knew that so long as I could hear the voices from the room next door, I was still alive. It was as though I was outside my own body watching this tragedy, yet unable to do anything about it. I was experiencing the cardiac survivor's worst nightmare.........the panic attack! However, I can happily announce that my perceptual machinery was in obvious need of repair that night for I managed to survive my terror and live to experience many more similar episodes over the next few years.

Panic attacks were a regular part of my life following my first heart attack, and for a year or two after the second one. I have no idea what precipitated them. I do not even know how long each one lasted. They hit from out of nowhere, spread their blanket of terror quickly, and then disappeared into a web of mystery. It seems kind of weird that I never experienced any pain during my panic attacks. There was just a tremendous amount of sweat. I was probably at greater risk of dying from dehydration than from heart failure. The

> ## What Do You Mean?
> ## Don't Panic...
> ## I Am Going To Die....Now!

most bizarre aspect was my complete inability to bring any rational thought to the situation. I would simply lose control. Of course, on reflection, I know that thoughts about dying won't kill me, and sweat isn't all that dangerous. However, such words of reason offer no comfort to the panic stricken. It seems impossible to short-circuit the process. Once it comes on, there appears to be no way to escape it. The panic has to run its course.

It has been more than twenty years since my last panic attack. I don't think about them much anymore, and it doesn't upset me to talk about them. However, those experiences confirmed for me that a heart attack doesn't only leave its physical mark. It is also a mind blower that leaves most survivors with some significant psychological challenges. It is not unusual for cardiac survivors to experience serious bouts of heightened anxiety and panic attacks. This seems to come with the turf. The intensity of worry may vary from person to person, but most of us go through a 'basket case' stage where worrying about our health amounts to a full-time occupation.

The time frame for physical recuperation is easily defined by the hospital stay and follow-up visits to the physician. The psychological trauma poses quite a contrast because of its ill-defined time frame. It may linger for just a few months or a lifetime. In fact, long after the physical repairs are complete, most survivors continue to struggle with psychological pain. An intense, persistent and completely intrusive form of worry can wear them down. The situation is made worse by the fact that usually there isn't much help readily available for their worry battle even though it will likely be their most difficult challenge.

> ## The Heart Heals Faster Than The Mind Because It Has No Memory

It is near impossible to avoid a battle with anxiety. A heart attack is a brutal signal that reminds you of your mortality..........with a thud! Once you experience a heart attack, there is no going back. The road you are walking is a dangerous one, and that reality causes anxiety. I am not sure anyone can understand just how intense that worry can become unless they have had to bear it. When the subject matter is your pending death, the anxiety level tends to be high. You are now very aware that your life has an end. So naturally, death becomes a bit more real, but it doesn't have to dominate you.

I know for myself the dark ages were definitely between the first and second heart attacks. I just could not escape the panic. Then, following my second coronary, I gradually recaptured control. Mind you, a day rarely goes by without that bloody heart condition coming into my mind and momentarily scaring the shit out of me. However, I have come to realize that my challenge is to contain the worry, not eliminate it by denying the reality of my circumstances. Similarly, you must learn to manage your anxiety because it is unlikely that you will recapture your quality of life without learning to effectively manage it. I do not deny that heart disease is a life-threatening disease. I also realize that facing up to this reality can generate prolonged bouts of anxiety. Nevertheless, this does not mean that you must remain a victim to anxiety. You may not be able to eliminate it, but you can learn to manage it.

The Great Worrier

It can be very difficult trying to find help for a worry problem. Many cardiac survivors first seek assistance from their physicians, but most medical practitioners are not properly trained to treat the psychological effects of a heart attack. Their vigorous training emphasizes the physical workings of the human coronary system, so they are less inclined to consider the mind as an important variable influencing cardiac health. Therefore, most believe the state of your health is reflected by such physical indicators as blood pressure, cholesterol and triglyceride levels, angiogram interpretations[10], blood tests and the degree of physical pain reported by you. Granted, some medical practitioners bring a holistic viewpoint to their practice, but they are the exception rather than the rule. Mainstream medicine, at least in the western world, is still dominated by persistent dualists who insist on treating the mind and body as separate entities. The physician mends the body while the psychologist heals the mind. However, the body and mind are so inter-dependent such dualism rarely brings the best results.

It is standard practice to quickly wean cardiac survivors from the medical system as their bodily functions return to normal. The specialists remove themselves from the scene once there is agreement on the diagnosis and all the physical interventions such as surgery are complete. The general practitioner or cardiologist may

---

10. Note the word interpretation. This is used purposefully because angiograms, particularly CT angiogram scans don't give a definitive reading on the degree of blockages in all the arteries. To some extent you are relying on the cardiologist's judgment.

hang around a bit longer to periodically monitor your vital signs and design a treatment plan to stabilize blood pressure, increase blood flow, prevent constipation, or treat any one of the other million inconveniences that the pharmaceutical companies eliminate with their 'drugs for everyone and everything.' However, if you decide on no drugs, in fairly short order you will be discharged from the medical system with a bottle of aspirin.[11] And the mental anguish? Sorry pal, that's your problem. So face the facts, you will have to rely on your own resources to a large extent if you are going to get control of your anxiety.

For Many Cardiac Survivors Anxiety Is A Bigger Problem Than Heart Disease

The Thought Police

Anxiety is not a life-threatening disease. Trust me. It only feels that way. Being anxious does not mean you are on the brink of death. It doesn't even mean you are going crazy. Everyone experiences anxiety from time to time. It gets the adrenaline flowing and helps you to be alert. Then you can react when a bear chases you. Anxiety only becomes a problem when you let it overwhelm you. The trick is to get in the driver's seat when you are confronted with anxiety. Better still, avoid its extreme forms. How do you do that? You must take control of your thoughts so you will stop compulsively monitoring every sensation that passes through your body.

Years ago, I was sitting in an airplane on my way to the west coast when a scary thought came into my head about an hour outside

---

11. Aspirin is certainly one of the in drugs for cardiac survivors. I take one every Monday, but many physicians and cardiac survivors believe it best to swallow a baby aspirin every day. Of course, as with any medication there are risks.

of Vancouver, "What would happen if I took a heart attack? Right now! No one can help me at 30,000 feet in the air.......I will die!" This thought made me really nervous, really fast. I started feeling light headed and quickly felt that familiar boulder settling into my stomach. There was a tingling sensation in my fingers and I thought, "I swear that is a pain I'm starting to feel in my chest. Jesus, I'm going to have another bloody heart attack!" [12]

> ## Think Catastrophe
> ## Feel Anxious

Who is in charge here? If it is going to be you, you better learn to get rid of thoughts like this fast. I grabbed my briefcase and got engrossed in some work that took a good deal of concentration. The anxious feelings passed in moments. Another reminder that the battle against anxiety is primarily a mental one. Anyone is bound to feel a significant degree of anxiety if they insist upon thinking in catastrophic ways. This is particularly the case with cardiac survivors who insist on hunting for symptoms of heart disease.

All cardiac survivors are bound to worry.[13] Unfortunately, they also have an extremely active imagination when it comes to interpreting bodily symptoms. The old expression, 'The mind plays tricks on us,' fits here. When any symptom is felt, most cardiacs jump to morbid conclusions about heart attacks and dying. This is especially the case for the first few months following their heart attack. Their tremendous fear of having another heart attack gets them caught up in a vicious circle. They are prone to think the bottom line, so letting their imagination run wild quickly leads to the gruesome.

---

12. An airplane is not a good place for a cardiac to think about his heart.......unless he is afraid of flying......then it keeps him from worrying about plane crashes.

13. I wonder how many cardiac champs end up with ulcers. I did.

- "Imagine if I take a heart attack driving my car...!"
- "Imagine if I need to have by-pass surgery....!"
- "Imagine if my blood pressure runs so high I take a stroke....!"
- "Imagine if my angina becomes unbearable....!"
- "Imagine if my condition deteriorates to the point where I experience a lot of pain before I die....!"

The Problem With 'imagine if' Thoughts Is They Never Let You Enjoy The Calm Before The Storm

---

It is not in the interest of your health to allow such threatening thoughts to roam unchallenged in your mind. For instance, when the thought, "Imagine if I take a heart attack right now," enters your head, answer it right away:

"What a silly thought. I am not about to take a heart attack. I feel fine and I will feel even better once I stop this stupid 'imagine if' game."

Alternatively, you may take a more emotional approach and yell:

"No! No! No! This is nuts! I'm not going to take a heart attack. What a stupid thought. No! No! No! It's not about to happen."

You have to select the style that best suits you, but passively allowing such worry thoughts to overwhelm you is not an option. With our medical histories we are bound to create some ambiguity when we focus on our physiology so we must not allow it to dominate our lives. All of these 'imagine if' thoughts hold just enough credibility to generate big time worry for you. Indeed, when such scary thoughts come into your head, it is quite natural to feel 'icky' all over your body.....dizzy, weak-kneed, tight stomach, mind outside of your body.....and all the rest of those unpleasant sensations that surround anxiety. When you think the worst, naturally you get really anxious and experience the accompanying unpleasant bodily sensations. They, in turn, are interpreted as heart related so the worry levels rise. It really is a vicious cycle that can quickly put you over the top on the fear index. It is difficult to determine which comes first, the unpleasant body sensations or the catastrophic thoughts, but the combination makes for unbearable feelings of extreme anxiety. Let's examine your physical sensations in more detail before learning some ways to control your thoughts about them.

Here A Symptom, There A Symptom, Everywhere A Symptom

Many cardiac survivors succumb to a unique compulsion during recovery. I call it chronic body monitoring. A chronic body monitor remains in a perpetual state of alertness so as to feel every internal movement in his body. This can be an unsettling pastime for anyone, but it is particularly threatening for cardiac survivors. They are monitoring their bodies to pick up advance warnings of their next heart attack. It is like being on death patrol. Many cardiacs end up crippled by anxiety because they experience so many physical symptoms which they translate as threats to their hearts. Unfortunately, the body is able to send off an endless number of signals. Most people pay little attention to these signals. For instance, if they perceive a kink in their back, they may pull their shoulder blades together or stretch their arms backwards and think no more about the fleeting sensation. Such is not the cardiac survivor's usual response. For us, each body signal, particularly between our abdomen and our neck, is a threat.....a threat that must be analyzed and diagnosed so we can be certain it is not an alarm for the Big One. You know the thought, "What's that? I never had that feeling before......is it in my chest?......My heart is going funny......something is going wrong. Should I do something? Is this serious?" The ante always escalates when we deny any experience with similar pain in the past, by deciding this is a unique kind of pain. This occurs when we think, "This one is really different. I never had this before. It's just not the same. The pain has never been so close to the centre of my chest. It is going to spread all over......these have got to be heart attack symptoms!" Such careful scrutiny often generates threatening interpretations that create other symptoms that cause further worry. It is an endless cycle originating with our compulsive need to monitor all of our body signals with extreme care.

> **Less Diligence Monitoring Symptoms**
> **More Diligence Monitoring Thoughts**

There is a lot of activity inside our bodies that is picked up by our brains. This only makes sense when you think of all the water, blood, electricity, nerve endings and muscles in the human body. They make for a lot of motion. Blood flows, the heart beats, water moves, gas builds up. The inside of the body is not sedentary. There is plenty of motion. For example, when you are sitting silently reading a book, you salivate and swallow at regular intervals. That physiological process actually generates a fair amount of motion within your body. However, you have no reason to monitor the saliva production, so you remain completely oblivious to the swallowing motion. In a similar vein, you frequently blink your eyes without being aware of doing so. Yet if you concentrate on saliva or blinking, you will quickly become acutely aware of these processes. Then you can become either amused, bored, or worried.

The average person experiences an assortment of twitches, temporary stiffness, and sudden jerks, along with a host of minor aches and pains, but they don't give much thought to them. That all changes when you take a heart attack. As I mentioned earlier, we are particularly sensitive to any sensations around our chests and abdomens. This can be a real hassle because the stomach is a particularly active organ with digestive responsibilities that come into play two or three times a day. The digesting process can include gas, tightness, bloating and other physiological sensations. These sensations don't get much of a reaction from the average person. Maybe a rub on the stomach, a burp or a grunt. Not so for cardiac survivors. Each sensation has to be assessed in depth, particularly if it originates in the stomach or chest.....well......or, the left arm, between the shoulder blades, the legs, the fingers......oh what the hell.....any part of the body. Look! We just believe that any of these sensations may be a concrete sign that our pending heart attack is about to hit! "This is it.......it feels like the Big One.........oh no!" A fleeting discomfort, a panic-ridden interpretation, and you are quickly saddled with intense anxiety.

To some degree, continual vigilance comes with the turf. It is part of the game even for a Cardiac Champ. I have been playing the compulsive monitoring game with varying degrees of intensity for the past twenty-five years. It is one of the few remaining scars of my recuperation. I joined the club right after my first heart attack when I started to compulsively monitor my pulse rate. I was convinced that my pulse rate was the key indicator for the general state of my health. A scary thought. I was gunning for seventy beats a minute, but I was always losing the bloody pulse before the minute was up. Finally, I gave up and looked for other signals to monitor. Trust me; there are hundreds to choose from. It is easy to start believing a dysfunctional heart is at the root of any discomfort. I can make an argument for virtually any physical discomfort being an early sign of impending doom. In fact, many years ago I actually had myself convinced that an irritating itch had its roots in my atherosclerosis.

It is crucial to realize that every physical pain or sensation you experience is not a sign that something is wrong, that you are in danger, or that you have an illness of significance. Your insides are in constant motion, yet every internal movement isn't a heart attack in disguise. Unfortunately, cardiacs seem to be very much aware of this motion and think the worst of it. I am not saying you should ignore all your bodily sensations. That would not be possible or wise, but it is also impractical to be running to the hospital with every tingle in your chest.

Anxiety....
You Can't Live Without It
So Learn To Live With It

The Cardiac Champ soon recognizes the importance of getting control over the propensity to monitor every bodily sound and movement. But how do you get that control? The starting point is to sort out dangerous pain from normal bodily sensations. You must learn to accept that not every ache, pain and injury is related to the cardiovascular system. Mind you, this is no easy task because heart pain is not as distinct as many people believe it to be. The popular description talks about an intense pain in the chest that radiates down the left arm and maybe up into the neck and jaw. It feels like the chest is being squeezed in a vice. That sounds like a fairly clear description, and if you are having that kind of pain, I urge you to get to the hospital quickly because you probably are having a heart attack. The problem is many people have heart attacks where the accompanying pain or discomfort doesn't fit this clear-cut description. For instance, some people actually suffer heart attacks without experiencing any chest pain. They only experience mild discomfort elsewhere in their bodies, or they notice no pain. There is simply no standard way for having a heart attack. You see, it really is your own unique experience, so enjoy the moment! Besides, even if there were a standard kind of heart attack pain, you would find a way to interpret the pain you feel as the standard kind. Let's face it. Any pain can get us going. We even react to the symptoms that accompany the common cold. It is not unusual to have muscle aches and pains when you have a common cold. They can create uncomfortable feelings in the chest, aches in the back, and a variety of unpleasant feelings in the area of the abdomen. What heart attack survivor hasn't translated these cold symptoms as the signals of a pending heart attack?

It is an endless struggle trying to determine which body signals warrant our attention. In many instances there may be no cause for alarm, yet we have all heard of cases where people ignored their bodies' messages and the results were fatal. Of course, the longer you live, the hazier your recollection of the actual feelings that accompanied your heart attack. That leaves you free to conclude that just about any feeling in your body is the early sign of a pending heart attack. So the orders for each day become stand on guard, monitor your symptoms, worry about them, and wait.

Intense vigilance is to be expected for the first few months following your heart attack. However, if this intensity persists, it will leave you feeling discouraged, frustrated and overwhelmed with a sense of hopelessness. In fact, it could leave you in a state of mental hell, so it is time to look at some techniques for controlling your compulsive monitoring behaviour. You may not be able to escape anxiety, but you certainly can learn to control it. The goal is to strike a balance between the inclination to compulsively worry and the cavalier attitude that leads one into doing things they later come to regret....... like doing push-ups to test the seriousness of chest pain. Confused? It sounds like I am telling you to take symptoms seriously, but ignore them. Not quite. I am suggesting it helps to be aware that a normal, healthy body has a significant amount of internal activity. Cardiac survivors are simply more aware of that activity than most people. The panic comes when you interpret the sensations in a threatening manner. That is what makes you uptight. So let's examine a program I designed to control your chronic monitoring and help you more accurately assess your bodily sensations.

VII
Get With The Program

Surviving a heart attack is enough to turn anyone into a nervous wreck, but a little insight can help you regain control. Chronic body monitors need a self-help program that allows them to escape the anguish that comes with interpreting every physical sensation as a coronary symptom. Much of the anxiety they experience stems from their worry thoughts about physiological sensations. The mind and the body conspire to burden the cardiac survivor with anxiety. To many, it appears as though the worry cycle begins with a physical symptom. However, our thought processes usually serve as the starter in developing our anxiety response. There is an exercise you can use to help you understand the role your thought processes play in creating anxious feelings. It highlights the power of suggestion. Sit up straight in a hard-backed chair. Close your eyes, but do not relax. In fact, allow your body to tighten up a bit and concentrate on your chest. Now use this thought pattern. Imagine there is a squeezing sensation across your chest. This causes the chest to tighten up. It may even become a little bit harder for you to breathe. It is possible the tightness you feel is the early sign of a heart attack.......all the signs seem to be there! Think hard about these feelings and sensations. If you hold such thoughts for a few moments, any number of symptoms are liable to show up in your body. That is, you actually 'will' some kind of physiological response from the inside of your chest cavity. Indeed, you worry about your symptoms so much that you actually generate more symptoms. It seems weird, but the worry, rather than your cardiovascular system, is actually the source of your discomfort.

Here is another example. You are having a particularly tough day so you are in a really negative space. You start thinking pessimistically about heart disease, angina, crippling surgery and other such cheery events. The negative thoughts put your body in overdrive leaving you with a bad case of the jitters. This condition is bound to generate any number of uncomfortable bodily sensations. The funny feelings give you the creeps, and in no time you are in a panic. Here the panic thoughts lead you to perceive unsettling bodily sensations which eventually cause more panic. Get it? An active imagination can play a significant role in escalating your anxiety levels.

Victim Logic......
I've Never Had That Gnawing Pain In My Toe Before
It Has To Be A Sign Of Poor Circulation
It Must Be Caused By My Heart Problems

I was the classic doom and gloom thinker after my first heart attack. I never let myself forget that heart attacks can kill. That focus helped to keep my mind filled with morbid thoughts. I spent hours planning for my family's future without me. I found it toughest at night-time. I would lie in bed thinking of the horrors my children would face following my imminent death. I could not fathom the life of a one year old and a three year old without a father, but saw it as my children's destiny. I spent hours trying to figure out ways to secure their financial future. This was a hell of a challenge since at that time I was living from payday to payday. I also dwelled on my guilt feelings which were easily conjured up when I thought of the major hassle I had caused for my wife. Remember, at the time, I believed my heart problems were solely the result of a lousy lifestyle dominated by cigarettes, late nights and fatty foods. It was not hard to conclude that had I never developed such 'self-destructive' habits, my family would have been spared the anguish.

I also spent a good portion of my time thinking about funeral arrangements. A real pick-me-up. I wasn't comfortable discussing my imminent funeral with anyone, so it remained mental homework. I thought out every last detail and even wrote up a plan. The plan included a unique message system for after I die. It resembled a dead man's Easter egg hunt. I had a file folder at home with all the information on my pension in it. I assumed my wife would look in it sometime after my death. So I left a note in it instructing her to look in another file that listed our bonds. That file had further instructions guiding her to another file with another note.....and on, and on. In no time I had invented all sorts of games to be played after my death. This kind of negative thinking and planning consistently generated enough anxiety to produce a collage of physical symptoms that perpetuated my worry cycle.

**Don't Be A Victim
Take Charge Of Your Thoughts**

A Bolt of Lightning

There are all sorts of things in your life you are able to change with a bit of effort and determination. By the same token, some things are beyond your influence. You only become a Cardiac Champ after you accept the conditions in your life over which you have no power. Your medical past is a good example. You have had a heart attack. There is not much you can do about that now. It is a fact, so accept it and get on with life. This is no easy task, but it can be done. Of course you got a lousy break, particularly if you are under fifty, but you can't moan about it for the rest of your life. I will concede, you are entitled to a period of mourning, but if it lasts for more than a few months, you are smothering yourself with too much pity. A doom and gloom approach keeps you stuck in the victim role. So get unstuck and concentrate on the things in your life that you can control.

Most people act as though they are helpless victims when it comes to their thoughts. They believe they have no control over the thoughts floating around in their minds. This is not true. You are not a victim who must accept everything that pops into your head. In fact, you can acquire the discipline needed to take charge of your thoughts. The starting point is to develop a realistic perspective on your physical condition. Once you have come to terms with reality on this count, you will be in a better position to challenge your self-defeating thoughts.

If You Can't Change It
Don't Dwell On It

This dramatic change came for me several months following my second heart attack. I remember the turning point well. I was sitting at my desk in work. For the hundredth time I was preoccupied with thoughts of my death. This time my mind was focused on the graphic details about how the embalmer should prepare my hair and face. Usually these sorts of thoughts made me nervous and sad, but for some reason this time I didn't get nervous and sad. I got mad! I got up from my chair, walked to the office door and shut it. I thought, "This is nuts......I can't go on living this way." I was talking out loud to myself. I started to give myself a lecture. It was a lecture that set me on a new journey. I wrote down:

I am going to die from some form of heart disease. In all likelihood a heart attack will do me in. In fact, since I have already had a couple of heart attacks my death will probably be premature. That thought doesn't turn me on. It's not fair, but who said life is supposed to be fair. There is no referee to make sure life is fair for everyone. There aren't even rules. Events just don't unfold as I wish or anyone else wishes. Some things I control. Some things control me. I got thrown a curve ....what a bitch. My heart disease is real, but it is only one part of my reality. I don't have to spend all my time thinking about it. I am not going to deny what happened to me. I accept it, but I also know I am a strong guy with loads of energy and a real zest for life. Of course, it's a bummer to know it will probably end a lot faster for me than for most people. But it hasn't ended yet. So I have to make the most out of whatever time I have left.

What's Important Is Not When You Will Die, But What You Are Going To Do Between Now And The Time You Do Die

---

What a breakthrough! I remember this whole scene as though it were yesterday. I was on a roll, and I knew it. I was finally coming to grips with my past by realizing that what counts is now. I had a choice here. Was I going to spend the rest of my days mourning my impending death or was I going to get some fun out of life? I chose fun.

You are bound to lead a miserable existence if you insist on dwelling on your heart disease and a gloomy future. A happy alternative is to live for the here and now. Figure out what you want, what you can do, and go for it. The rest? Learn to accept what you can't control or change. Then you can focus all your mental energy on the positive aspects of your life. This realistic, but positive, attitude toward your heart disease sets you on the road to gaining control over negative and self-defeating thoughts. You will gradually develop the determination to challenge any negative thoughts you have regarding your health. To effectively manage your anxiety, it is crucial for you to develop the skill to aggressively challenge negative thoughts.

Fantasy............Sex Only Please

The wandering mind poses a potential danger for cardiac survivors because their fantasies tend to focus on heart issues. It is great to have an active fantasy world when the subject is sex, but it is not so great when the subject is your heart. Therefore, you must make an effort to control the content of your fantasy world. Not a very exciting prospect, but even Cardiac Champs must be diligent about random thoughts. If I spend too much time daydreaming, nine times out of ten I end up thinking not about sex, but about emergency rooms, heart surgery, funerals and similar deathly topics. Such fears are always just below the surface, and you are better off to leave them there. That means learning different techniques to prevent such dreary subject matter from emerging into your thoughts. We all fantasize, daydream and think random thoughts. The trick is to make sure the daydreams are about grandiose schemes of success, sexual pleasures, plans for spending our lottery winnings and other similar fun topics.

It is particularly important to control the wanderings of your thoughts at bedtime. It can be pretty scary when you turn out the lights and settle into bed for the night. The quiet and stillness of the night induce a wonderful sense of relaxation for most people, but it can be the most anxious time for Cardiac Champs. The darkness and quiet create a very lonely setting where it is easy to conjure up the horrors of our recent medical past. The ghosts of the night become all our fears around heart disease. Fight it! As soon as you become aware of a doomsday thought on your mind, replace it with a happy one. There is no magic process. It is simply a matter of taking control of your mind and thinking about your golf game, vacations, food, sex, happy times with your family, a book you are reading, or any other pleasant subject. These pleasant thoughts must surface to overpower the fearful ones. Eventually this shift in thought becomes an automatic response. It really does work. The payoff is getting a decent night's sleep. I will talk about sleeping problems in more detail later.

The Happy Neurotic

On the one hand, I am telling you to challenge your panic thoughts, but on the other hand, I caution you to be aware that the source of your pain may be organic. This apparent contradiction is troubling, but it is a reality for those with heart disease. When the body breaks down in some area it gives off a warning signal, usually in the form of pain. So you cannot ignore the fact that the pain you are experiencing may well be the product of a malfunctioning heart. Maybe the arteries are so badly blocked that life-saving oxygen is having a tough time getting around the body. That is scary. Conversely, it is equally scary to think that you should trot off to the hospital with every symptom. Yes Mabel, we do have a dilemma here.

I am not suggesting you should never listen to your body, but there is no clear-cut formula for determining when your symptoms are the sign of a real heart attack or simply another false alarm. This is the kind of ambiguity most of us encounter from time to time for the rest of our lives. Are the concerns unfounded? Who knows? Certainly in many instances there is obviously no cause for alarm because you survived. But in some instances, you may be facing fatal signs. After all, you likely have some blocked arteries and may suffer from spasms. However, you have to strike some balance or you'll go crazy.

| The Big Challenge....
Ignore Most Pain, But Don't
Misinterpret The Real Thing |
| :---: |

This cardiac recovery business can be tough. I know it is a monumental task to accurately interpret the messages of bodily sensations after you have experienced a heart attack. Indeed, with each pain you must go through a 'heart-wrenching' analysis of whether or not this is it. I would love to be able to say, "Look, the best advice is to simply monitor your body with care. When you feel pain, locate where it is coming from, and then take a moment to think about it. If after a few moments you still think the discomfort is an early symptom of a heart attack, get to the hospital." This sounds like sensible advice, but it poses some real problems. For one thing, if all cardiacs followed it, the hospitals of the world would be overflowing with 'wannabe' patients. Indeed, some of us would be visiting the hospital a few times a week or maybe every day. Such diligence would create another problem. Ninety percent of cardiac survivors would be suffering from dysfunctional depression. So if for no other reason but our own sanity, we must strengthen our pre-hospital analysis and develop some confidence in our decision making skills. The bottom line? Unfortunately, it is a judgment call. However, don't give up the battle just yet. Hopefully the strategy that follows will help you to establish a comfort zone with your judgment calls.

I have had significant trouble finding my comfort zone with bodily sensations. I am inclined to focus on my symptoms with a great deal of vigour. In fact, until recently it was my major downfall. I, like most survivors, perceived very similar symptoms over and over again, but failed to recognize the repetition. Of course, it was a habit that prevented me from gaining the confidence of past experience. Since I always thought I was experiencing the symptom for the first time, I believed my survival was at stake each time. This left me experiencing the same level of anxiety each time the same symptom came around. It took me a number of years to recognize this inclination to interpret every symptom as a unique one. Once I discovered my propensity to forget that I had survived a given symptom, I decided to develop a monitoring system to track the symptoms I experienced each day. After using this system for several weeks, it was quite easy to develop my very own symptoms profile.

I began my new adventure with symptoms by just writing them down. Sure enough I soon noticed the same ones turning up over and over again. So I began to record them in a more methodical fashion. After some experimenting, I settled on the design outlined in The Symptoms Chart. It is an easy chart to use. The primary column on the left side of the page is headed 'Perceived Symptoms.' To start, you only make entries in this column. List all the symptoms you observe for a couple of weeks. They will likely vary from a pain in the groin, to a nervous stomach, to foot cramps. Be precise. Describe each symptom in four words or less. Be sure to continue this exercise until you are certain you have listed all the symptoms, even if it takes a month; you don't want to miss any. You may be surprised to discover that you experience only ten or fifteen distinct symptoms even though it feels like a couple of hundred. Nevertheless, the important point is to keep a note pad handy at both work and home and mark them all down.

Once you have identified all your symptoms, decide on the phrase or group of words you will use to describe each symptom. Then re-list them under the 'Perceived Symptoms' column as shown in The Symptoms Chart. Now you are ready to use the columns headed by the names of the days of the week. Use these columns to the right of the perceived symptoms column to tick off how often you experience a specific symptom during each day. Simply put a check mark in the appropriate box each time you experience the symptom.

THE SYMPTOMS CHART

Perceived Symptoms	S	M	T	W	T	F	S
Stomach Ache							
Nervous Stomach							
Stomach Cramps							
Tingling Sensations							
Feeling Dizzy							
Spaced Out Feeling							
Fast Heart Beat							
Heart Beat Too Slow							
Weak All Over							
Headache							
Blurred Vision							
High Chest Pain							
General Chest Pain							
Localized Chest Pain							
Numb Left Arm							
Pain Back/Shoulders							
Groin Pain							
Itchy arm, back, leg etc.							
Legs Feel Weak							
Leg Cramp							
Foot Cramp							
General Malaise							
Feel About to Faint							
Who Knows What It Is							

You will notice that the last symptom listed on my chart is 'Who Knows What It Is.' You may find this a handy label. I included 'Who Knows What It Is' to ensure I always recorded symptoms that were difficult to describe but were causing uncomfortable feelings in my body. I think the early signs of depersonalization are what usually fell into this category. The important point is to include all the symptoms you experience, so when in doubt include it under 'Who Knows What It Is.'

This neurotic dedication to tracking symptoms may seem to be a self-defeating process. Not so. It is actually a very important step in coming to grips with your symptomology. A concrete approach to symptom counting gives you very important feedback. A systematic data collection system helps you see all the symptoms you overcome, or at least survive, each day. This visual aid is good for your confidence. As well, the recording helps you to identify patterns. You will begin to realize that many of the symptoms you think you are experiencing for the first time are actually regular visitors to your body. Furthermore, it becomes self-evident that many are not life-threatening. For instance, if after four weeks you find that you had a feeling of general malaise six times, and a nervous stomach seventeen times, but had no heart attack, it makes it easier for you to accept that these symptoms are probably not life-threatening for you. Of course, judgment still comes into play. Recording symptoms does not eliminate the challenge of trying to determine what pain requires medical attention versus what is the product of your anxiety. I am not suggesting that crunching pain across your chest should simply be recorded on the symptoms chart while ignoring the option of visiting a physician. However, the symptoms chart will help you establish a comfort zone where many more symptoms are recognized as the clear product of anxiety rather than anything that requires a physician's attention.

The Terror Leaves When You Take Charge Of Your Symptoms

I started to systematically monitor my symptoms shortly after my second heart attack. The symptoms chart was an immense help. I listed every symptom I felt for several weeks. It only took a couple of weeks for me to see that there was a clear pattern. I had fourteen recurring symptoms, but four totally dominated me. They were feeling spaced out, believing my legs were wobbly, a general malaise, and a perpetual nervous stomach. These were the main culprits that posed a constant threat to my sanity. I think most cardiac survivors have similar chart patterns where three or four symptoms dominate their feelings. However, the dominating symptoms will vary from individual to individual. Some experience the sensation of their heart pounding too hard or their pulse stopping for prolonged periods. Others frequently experience a feeling of weakness all over that is interpreted as a sign of impending death. Regardless, the sensations are often so powerful it is nearly impossible not to believe that something terrible is about to happen.

It is hard to avoid a state of panic when you are being bombarded by so many symptoms, but the symptoms chart can help you bring some order to this chaos. The use of the chart helps the survivor to gain some confidence by seeing the pattern. Using the chart will not eliminate all of the terror you feel when attempting to interpret the many symptoms you experience. However, it will help you gradually develop a sense of power over your symptoms. It helps you move out of the victim mode. It also prepares you to more effectively handle the next step in symptom management. That is, trying to determine the appropriate response to any given symptom.

Your symptoms can leave you too afraid to resist unless you learn to challenge them. The decision-making process for responding to symptoms doesn't lend itself to the strict application of logic. It is more a matter of trying to balance risk with lifestyle choices. In the end, you are probably best served by using your head, but following your heart. The objective is to find a comfort zone that balances the need to challenge with the need for responsible caution. My comfort zone allows me to push enough to conquer most of my symptoms and enjoy a vigorous life. The balance is found at some vague point where I allow the reality of my medical history to take precedence. Here I accept the message my body is giving me as a warning signal. It is at those times that I slow down, take an Ativan, or on the rare occasion, visit a nurse to get my blood pressure checked. You have to make the choices.

You will only obtain peace of mind when you significantly reduce the time spent monitoring your body. However, it also helps when you develop some confidence around interpreting your body signals. Cardiac Champs are unique because they find a safe point on the risk scale when it comes to feelings of discomfort and pain. They make a decision that certain kinds and levels of pain are to be tolerated, while recognizing that they may pay with their lives for even one wrong call. So, there is a point, and it is largely a gut feeling, where they will not hesitate being rushed to the hospital. Persist! Somewhere in your perceptions there is a comfort zone that will define the balance between being a neurotic fool and ignoring it all. Cardiac Champs have no desire to be chronic visitors to the hospitals, but they also have no desire to drop dead on the sidewalk.

I am sure there have been Cardiac Champs in the past that died because they were not sufficiently vigilant about certain symptoms. It can happen. You will have to decide which risks you are prepared to take to maintain the quality of life you believe is essential. I must take some degree of risk to maintain my happy, active lifestyle. I have decided to do so because I believe it is worth it. This does not mean that I ignore all my symptoms....just most of them. Believe me, I am a real body watcher, but I have found my point of equilibrium. I have gradually developed a confidence that leaves me feeling that most of my discomfort is a product of anxiety rather than blocked arteries. This optimism allows me to neurotically enjoy the wonders of life, rather than spend all of my time neurotically sitting in a physician's waiting room or the emergency department of a local hospital.

Worry Mates

The worry game is best played in partnership. You may be a big fan of the Lone Ranger, but remember, he was no anxiety neurotic so he was better equipped to go it alone. It is a self-defeating strategy to play the hero and tell no one about the psychological pain that comes with your fear of death. This doesn't mean you should smother everyone you know with your mental luggage, but it is therapeutic to have a couple of people in your life with whom to share your pain. I say a couple of people because the anxiety-ridden cardiac can be quite draining when on a 'let's share my worries' rampage. Once the 'worry can' is opened, it may be difficult to close it. You need a few supporters so they can spell each other off while they listen to you moan.

A Neurotic? Maybe.
A Lonely Neurotic?
Never!

The spouse can play a very important role in helping the cardiac survivor to conquer anxiety. S/he can help the cardiac express his feelings and more importantly, help put them in perspective. Possibly, the partner's most important role is helping the cardiac accept feedback regarding the reporting of symptoms. In the early stages of symptom monitoring, cardiac survivors are notorious for distorting perceptions of their own symptoms. The partner can help by serving as a source for reality checks. I used to think every symptom I perceived was potentially deadly and definitely being experienced for the first time: "This is it......I know this one is different......I am going to die!" Anyone who has lived with a cardiac survivor for a couple of weeks has heard this line. It is the common cry of the cardiac. So the spouse can gradually help the survivor recognize that the symptoms are neither deadly nor appearing for the first time.

> **When Your Mate Moans Too Much**
> **Just Tell The Asshole**
> **To Sit Down And Take A Nitro**

A cardiac's spouse can be a tremendous source of encouragement, but let me warn you, being a cardiac cheerleader is a difficult job. There is a lot of neurotic moaning by the survivor during the initial stages of recovery. Living with someone who is voicing perpetual panic can be a terrifying experience. Ready or not, you become the sounding board for your loved one as they try to cope with all of the body signals that accompany anxiety. It is not very comforting to have someone crawling around the house groaning, "I think this is the Big One!" Actually, it is a dreadful scene to witness, so keeping all of your anguish bottled up inside is not good for you. You must share your fears. You need support too. Indeed, it is not uncommon for the spouse to be even more nervous about the future than the survivor. This is a normal reaction. So you must speak up, and that includes sharing your feelings and fears with your cardiac survivor.

The idea is not to clam up the cardiac victim, but have him or her understand that you also worry. The role reversal may be helpful. Cardiac Champs grasp the opportunity to empathize and understand the needs of the significant people in their lives. They always have enough emotional energy to look after the needs of their loved ones. Indeed, true Cardiac Champs welcome the opportunity to witness the other side of the coin knowing they have a tendency to get too caught up in their own struggles.

A final word on anxiety. You can't do anything about the fact that you have had a heart attack. That event will be a part of your medical history forever, but you have a big say in how you are going to react to your medical history. Heart attacks often kill, so when you survive this life-threatening situation, it is bound to penetrate the core of your emotions. The threat of the Big One is there. Your challenge? To ensure that the threat doesn't become the major focus of your life. It is impossible to live a happy, vigorous life when you are stricken with persistent, nagging, gut wrenching, chronic anxiety. Such a cross no one should have to carry, and remember, it is your decision as to whether or not you carry it.

VIII
I'm Not Mad, Jerk!

It was four days after my cardiac arrest. I was out of the intensive care unit. My new digs were a private room on the coronary ward. It was infuriating to be back in the hospital with more heart problems. I was mad! I hated being so vulnerable and dependent on other people. I did not know the attending physician. I hated the food. I could not sleep. I was upset, frustrated and afraid, but most of all angry. It wasn't just having another heart attack that was making me so angry. I responded with anger to most things that upset me. Looking back now, I realize I was angry quite a lot during my first forty years of life. Strangely, it wasn't a very visible anger that got expressed in any obvious way. I was never much of a yeller, never violent or even physically aggressive. Granted, I was always extremely competitive, and could certainly keep up with the best when it came to arguments, but the real action was hidden inside. Inside there was not only a competitive spirit with a dose of verbal aggression, there was a burning rage! A rage that had been with me for decades. A rage that was about to surface as the opponent in one hell of a psychological battle.

I was in the hospital about a week when a good friend came to visit me. It was what I label a high impact visit because it set the stage for some dramatic changes. My friend was a psychologist who knew me well. His visit was memorable because he confronted me with my anger at just the right moment. This was not a new topic of discussion for either of us as we both acknowledged being angry young men. However, this time it was different for me. There was an impact! I never did find out why he chose to hassle me on a day when I was flat on my back waiting for the Big One. I guess he felt I was so vulnerable I would be susceptible to guidance. Anyway, he certainly laid it on the line. Now, like me, this buddy is a psychologist so his comments were dressed up in that psycho-babble no one understands, but in plain English he more or less said, "You are an angry sonofabitch. You have always been angry. It is probably a large part of the reason you are lying in that bed. That unexplained, intensive, raging anger is destroying you. It has to go."

We talked a lot that evening. I knew the gig was up. It was time to put out the burning fire of rage. This conversation marked the beginning of my concentrated battle against the most destructive emotion of all. Note, I use the term battle. It was a battle, and it lasted three or four years, but in the end 'calm' was the victor, so I live to tell the story.

I did not give much thought to my personality after my first heart attack. Like most, I viewed the heart attack strictly as a physical event. To me, the recuperation period was simply a time for regaining my physical strength. So I followed an excellent diet, stopped smoking and exercised on a regular basis. That was not enough. I have since realized the important influence psychological factors, particularly anger and anxiety, have on the rehabilitation process. After my second heart attack I chose a reasonable diet, the occasional smoke, regular exercise and a direct hit on anger! I haven't had the third heart attack. A coincidence? Maybe, but the calm in place of the anger has sure produced a nice glow. Oh, how I wish I had attended to my psychological well-being after that first one. If I had done so, I probably would not have been in cardiac arrest less than three years later. It is so important to gain control of the most dangerous emotion of all..........anger.

Anger is a very powerful emotion, but you can get control of it. You must. I cannot over-emphasize this point. I firmly believe that persistent, unresolved anger is a major contributing factor to heart disease which is why no cardiac survivor should remain a slave to it. I would not be alive today if I had not learned to handle my anger. I do not believe being an anxiety-ridden neurotic will kill you. However, the story is not the same with anger. It is a killer. We all agree there is no single cause for heart disease, but I would list anger as a significant contributing factor.

Anger And Healthy Hearts Do Not Mix

There is an incredible amount of research being done throughout the world on the human cardiovascular system. Scientists are seeking to discover the causes of heart attacks so they can figure out how to prevent them. This is an astronomical scientific challenge because of the complexities associated with the development of heart disease. The puzzle is complex because human beings are complex. The Big One is the result of many factors interacting at the same time in changing circumstances upon unique individuals, so there is much we still don't understand about the event. There may well be dozens of causal factors. It is a bit of a mystery, and most of the human race has a hard time coping with mysteries. The simpler the answer, the better we like it. Perhaps this explains why the more straightforward explanations for heart disease and the ways to avoid it are the ones most likely to penetrate the public's consciousness. This turns the spotlight on the physical dimensions rather than the psychological ones. New contributing factors are added from time to time, but the emphasis has always been on the physical. At first, medical practitioners were focusing on blood pressure, family history and diabetes as the primary causes of heart disease. Then poor diet, lack of exercise and smoking were added to the equation. It is only in more recent years that some researchers have begun to hypothesize that an individual's personality may also have a significant impact on heart health.

The history of heart disease research confirms the fact that most studies emphasize factors associated with physical health. For instance, the effects of smoking on the development of heart disease in a given population has received significant study by researchers. Similarly, diet, blood pressure and obesity all receive a good share of attention in the research literature. In contrast, the relationship between personality factors and coronary health still receives scant attention, although there have been a couple of major studies by medical researchers over the past few decades. This discrepancy is easily explained when you realize that concrete matters more easily lend themselves to research. Many researchers may now accept that personality is linked to the development of coronary problems, but it is very difficult to research and draw conclusions about these more abstract aspects of human life. For instance, it is a lot easier to study smoking behaviour than anger. It is easier to define smoking behaviour. It is easier to observe it, and it is easier to measure it. So smoking gets studied because it is a manageable variable. The same can be said for blood pressure, weight and even eating habits. These characteristics lend themselves to definition, measurement and statistical formulas. So it is not surprising that researchers select smoking behaviour, fat intake, blood pressure and exercise for their studies. Furthermore, since the focus of research generally dictates the substance of treatment and prevention programs, it follows that most in cardiac care will emphasize the physical aspects over the psychological ones.

The imbalance remains even though physical variables by themselves fail to fully account for the high rates of heart disease. We all know smokers who rarely exercise or people who are not into a balanced diet who still live to a ripe old age. Similarly, there are thousands, maybe millions, of nonsmokers who are reasonably active and eat nutritious food, but who still acquire heart disease and die from heart attacks. This group is discounted as a minority by the health industry, but they are a significant group that should be studied more carefully by researchers. In fact, they probably possess the key to the mystery box that holds the secret to avoiding premature heart disease. That secret cannot be described solely in physical terms. Psychological factors must be examined in conjunction with the physical aspects if we are to unlock the secret to healthy living.

I am not suggesting you should ignore nutrition, exercise, smoking habits and other similar behaviours. They count, but you must also pay attention to your personality, and I think anger warrants special attention. I believe many, if not most, cardiac survivors are very angry people. The anger may not be expressed overtly, but the rage burns within them. If you are one of these people and expect to survive, I urge you to read the following section about anger with great care. Let me be blunt. Getting rid of your anger, whether you hold it in or express it physically, is crucial to maintaining good health. There is no room for denial here. You need to take a long hard look at how you manage your anger.

The Beast Of Anger

Anger is an emotion that surfaces in response to a combination of events. It is an end product. In most cases anger is rooted in the belief that life should unfold in a manner pleasing to us. This attitude suggests that the world around us and all the events in it should be under our control. Such an attitude is bound to leave us hostile and bitter when life follows its own course. And since life events often do follow their own unique course, angry people can be left in a state of perpetual frustration which does nothing but intensify their anger.

There are some circumstances where anger is a fitting emotional response, but usually it does more harm than good. It is certainly no friend to the cardiovascular system, even though many cardiac survivors are consumed by destructive feelings of rage. Anger hangs around with a bad crowd. It generates unpleasant accompanying emotions such as frustration, intolerance, and fear. Even the physical features associated with excessive anger are unpleasant. Much of your body tightens, your heart beat increases, blood pressure goes up and you sweat. In fact, its physical effects can be so strong that they leave you feeling as though you are literally going to physically explode. It seems certain that persistent anger takes its toll on the body. I remember well when anger still had me in its grip. Sometimes I was so angry with what had taken place during the day at work, that while driving home it felt like my chest was in some kind of a vice. At times, my reaction was so strong it created physical pain. Anger is that powerful an emotion. Obviously such emotions and physical sensations are not pleasant for anyone, whether they act out their anger or suppress it.

> ## The Only Person Who Can
> ## Make You Angry
> ## Is Yourself

Many cardiac survivors think it is not their fault that they feel so much anger. We have all heard the pleas, "How can anybody keep their cool with that jerk!" or "I just can't stop myself!" or "It is impossible not to get angry when that happens!" Oh yes it is. You are in charge here, but an internalized sense of helplessness stops you from realizing your own power. Get with the program! You are not the helpless victim of some external force known as anger.

It is not an external situation or some person who is beyond your control that is making you angry. You make yourself angry. You will never conquer your anger if you allow yourself to live under the illusion that you are powerless over your reactions to people and situations. You cannot control all situations nor people's behaviour, but you can certainly control your reaction to them. So the next time you blow your cool, go stand in the corner and repeat ten times, "I make myself angry, and I am going to stop doing so." If you repeat this truism often enough, you may eventually come to believe it.

Everyone experiences anger at different points in their life. That is normal. It is healthy to get angry once in a blue moon when some situation rubs you the wrong way. Such well-placed anger does not reflect an angry personality. The angry person is the one who has persistent feelings of frustration and disappointment along with a desire to lash out. With the angry person these feelings surface with most situations that do not go exactly as planned. Unfortunately many, if not most, cardiac survivors seem to fit into this angry person category. Their anger is not a new and specific response stemming from the frustration of having had a heart attack. You will rarely find a person whose anger button has been pushed solely by the fact that they have had a heart attack. Most survivors who have that burning rage or persistent anger will discover, if they look, that it is a well ingrained personality trait, and their response to the heart attack is merely another example of their inability to control or rid themselves of it.

Angry people lose their cool fast. They become upset over the small stuff. They overreact to minor aggravations like being stopped by a red light when in a hurry. They get frustrated and often angry with line-ups at checkout counters. The angry person is overpowered by an incredible urge to make the smallest of issues a big deal. The intensity seems to be always turned up. This is often evident when personal opinion is on the line. It is as though the angry person views every verbal exchange as a battle. It is near impossible to have a simple exchange of ideas or opinions with such people. You may recognize this kind of anger in yourself if you are often told, "Everything seems to turn into an argument." That kind of a comment is a signal that you are too concerned with making your points and winning arguments. A key to crawling out from under the control of anger is to recognize that you don't have to win every debate, and the whole world doesn't have to accept your point of view. As an old sage once said, "It is not so bad to be a bit full of shit once in a while."

The survivor who has a strong need for control is bound to have a rocky ride after the Big One. Heart attacks have a way of making people feel like they have no control over their lives. They certainly are lousy confidence boosters for control freaks. Ironically, this vulnerability often leaves the victim even madder than he was before the heart attack. Once the angry cardiac senses he is not in control of his destiny, he experiences a build-up of rage. I remember, prior to my second heart attack, often feeling extreme anger for no apparent reason. The problem was not only my health. I felt my world was not unfolding the way it should because I wasn't living in the city I wanted to be in, and I was getting little satisfaction from my work life. Not end of the world circumstances, but conditions that left me feeling I had no control over my life. That made me mad! Conditions were not to my liking, and I believed life should unfold my way. It was as though I thought the world was somehow against me when things went wrong.

Angry People Are Control Freaks

Angry people usually see the world as a hostile place so respond to it in a confrontational, belligerent and aggressive manner. Naturally if you believe the world is basically hostile, you will have a tendency to respond in a hostile fashion. The healthy route is to let go of the anger. The idea of letting your anger go sounds easy enough, but it poses a major challenge for the anger beast. Hopefully, your heart disease is an additional source of motivation. The stakes are somewhat higher now that you have had a heart attack. If you allow this free-floating anger to dominate you much longer, you just may die. So for the sake of your survival, it is time to take on your anger. This means starting to accept that the little things, or big things, in life won't always go your way. The impatience, the urge to have complete control, and the unrelenting desire to have things turn out the way you think they should, can gradually give way to a go-with-the-flow attitude. It is chill out time!

There are a few other traits we must identify to complete our portrait of the beast of anger. Angry people argue more than most and rarely, if ever, exhibit a self-deprecating quality. They are also much more likely to talk aggressively, loudly, and a lot. Angry people's inclination to view the world as a hostile place forces them to be always alert and fighting for control. Their excessive competitiveness shows through in most avenues of life. In sports, it usually manifests itself as an uncontrollable drive to win. With interpersonal relationships, it is more likely to manifest itself as extreme aggression or the need to be the more dominant party at all times in intimate relationships.

Does this personality profile sound like you? If so, you have a lot of work to do.......on yourself. This is not the portrait of a nice dude. So shape up. It is time for a major personality overhaul. This is going to be a long project so it is best to start now. Indeed, the best time to start is while you are still in hospital. That way we get you while you are still vulnerable so more likely to agree to fundamental change. However, it is not too late even if you have left the hospital. The important thing is to start now. Here is what you have to do:

1. Acknowledge that you are an angry person.
2. Find yourself an anger helper.
3. Identify your anger buttons.
4. Replace your angry thoughts with new calm ones.

Jerk, You Are Mad

The number one step in coming to grips with anger is to acknowledge its presence inside you. No one lets go of their anger so long as they continue to deny its existence. The questionnaire on the next page was designed to help you measure the degree of anger floating around in your personality. Read each statement once; then answer it right away. **Don't labour** over the statements. It will be more helpful if you give a spontaneous, honest answer. For each question that you answer 'rarely,' mark 1, for each question that you answer 'often,' mark 2, and for each question that you answer 'very often,' mark 3. Add up the totals for each column. These three totals added together will give your overall score. The highest possible score is 45 and the lowest is 15. The overall score is the important indicator, but it is worth reviewing your individual responses. One or two responses alone do not tell you much about yourself. However, certain patterns start to emerge when you group the responses. For instance, you may want to examine your reactions to feedback if questions 2, 10, 13 and 15 generated a 'very often' response. Similarly, I would want

The Anger Barometer

	1 Rarely	2 Often	3 Very Often
1. I argue with people at home	____	____	____
2. I feel people overreact to me	____	____	____
3. It bugs me when people disagree with me	____	____	____
4. I find myself out of control	____	____	____
5. I get angry watching television	____	____	____
6. I argue with waiters, attendants, sales clerks, etc.	____	____	____
7. I feel good using put-downs	____	____	____
8. I have negative feelings toward many people	____	____	____
9. I get mad at referees while watching sporting events	____	____	____
10. I feel people are out to get me	____	____	____
11. Situations arise where it takes all my energy to control my anger	____	____	____
12. I criticize people	____	____	____
13. People tell me to stop yelling	____	____	____
14. It upsets me when my opinion is not accepted by others	____	____	____
15. People tell me to calm down	____	____	____
TOTAL	____ +	____ +	____

to re-examine how I conversed with people if I responded 'often' to questions 1, 3, 6 and 14.

If your overall score is under 20, you are probably a fairly low key person when it comes to anger. If you scored from 20 to 35, you are encouraged to take a serious look at how you are dealing with the normal trials and tribulations of life. If your score is over 35, it is a good indication that your anger button is overactive and probably not doing you much good. However, I invite those cardiac survivors scoring over 30 to join the Cardiac Champs' march against anger. It is a rough journey, but you can successfully complete it if you take it step by step.

Your responses to the questionnaire may help you recognize the intensity of your anger, but that is only a starting point. It is also helpful to share your responses with some people you trust.

Talk with a few folks who have to deal with you on a daily basis. Encourage them to speak candidly about your anger. Also, take more careful notice of how you react to unpleasant situations. Such vigilant observation of your reactions is an important exercise for self-awareness. Heightened self awareness helps you own up to your anger. True self-knowledge is essential if you are to overcome the control anger has over your life. Reflect.

I have been stressing the importance of acknowledging your anger because you will only conquer it once you admit it has you in its grasp. However, this does not mean you must understand its origins. Many people try to delve into their inner personalities once they discover that they have an anger problem. They want to relate it to something in their childhood, a traumatic event, or having hung around with the wrong people. I question the value of such an approach. You don't need ten years of psychotherapy to get rid of your anger. This kind of soul-searching can be self-defeating because it encourages you to latch onto excuses. It may help you understand how you got to where you are now, but it also helps you to rationalize your self-defeating behaviours. You may even conclude, "I can't do anything about my anger. It is the result of my early childhood. It is my father's fault." Such drivel encourages you to avoid taking responsibility for your own failings. The outcome is usually no change.

> ## It Doesn't Matter Where Your Anger Comes From So Long As It Goes

If nothing else, fear forced me to re-examine my style of living after my second heart attack. It was obvious that by itself the physical approach to rehabilitation had not done me much good after my first heart attack. I was still in deep trouble with my health, and once my friend spoke to me in the hospital about my free-floating anger, I knew it was a big part of the problem. Funny thing. I never hit people, threw things, or even yelled much, but I knew inside there was a burning rage: a destructive force which I gradually recognized as a major contributor to the deterioration of my arterial system. It was becoming increasingly evident that anger more than anything else kept me tense, pumped up, frustrated, and in constant turmoil. It wasn't simply a matter of being pissed off about having heart attacks so young. I knew there was more there. I had been angry most of my life. I began to realize that I wasn't going to survive much longer without some big changes. I didn't spend much time sorting out my past. I knew it was the present that had to change. I had completed step one by acknowledging that I was an angry person. It was a giant step forward.

Calm For Hire

Self-awareness is a good starting point, but it is only a start. The next step is to eat some humble pie by sharing your self-awareness with others so you can enlist their support. It is very important for you to talk about your anger. You need a soul mate who understands the importance of your gaining control over your anger. So tell someone. This revelation may come as a surprise to your confidante if your method of dealing with anger is primarily suppression. Of course, if you are the kind of person who constantly yells and screams or who hits out at people, you will have no trouble convincing others that you have an anger problem. Whether you wear the rage on your sleeve or bottle it up deep in your guts, enlisting the assistance of others is essential. I know, owning up to our shortcomings is a humbling experience, but most angry people can use a good dose of humility. Besides, such a confession sets the stage for others to feel comfortable giving you some honest feedback regarding your progress in the battle against anger. Give people who care about you a chance to help. Of course, you want to be selective about whom you choose to hear this bit of news about yourself. If you are married, you may decide to enlist your spouse. Or maybe you will feel more comfortable telling a good friend. It is your choice, but I would discourage you from picking one of your workmates as your confidante. It is usually a good idea to keep your psychological struggles out of the workplace.

Once you have selected your anger helper, it is wise to set a very important ground rule. It should be understood that you are not going to deal with your anger when you are angry with your helper, or your helper is angry with you. That would not make for a very level playing field given your vulnerability with the helper. Make an agreement that stipulates when a situation reaches the boiling point, you will declare yourself to the friend or partner. Here you simply say, "I'm getting mad" or "This isn't going to work -- I'm leaving," and remove yourself from the situation. It is not the anger helper's role to exploit your vulnerability when the two of you are in conflict.

Alright, once you have owned up to your anger and found yourself an anger helper it is time to start the real hard work.

The Anger Buttons

You will not make much progress if your anger management program consists of nothing more than thinking, "I've got to stop getting mad" every time you respond in an angry way to a person or a situation. A more methodical approach is needed to bring about lasting change. It is very difficult to maintain self-awareness and work toward change if you do not follow a systematic strategy. It helps to start by identifying the people and situations that make you angry. This knowledge will alert you to the cues that signal your advancing anger. Who are the people who seem to most often press your anger button? Is it a boss, a workmate, your banker, a friend of your child's, or even your own child? Maybe it is all of these people plus many more. What about situations where you become angry? For instance, having to wait for service, losing at a game, the dog not coming when called, may all be situations that regularly get an angry response from you. It will take a bit of work to discover the exact sources of your anger, but the effort is worthwhile. Knowing the sources will give you direction and a focus for practising new responses. You may also want to ask your anger helper what he or she thinks makes you angry. No doubt, the answer will expand the list.

The Anger Buttons Checklist will help you identify some of the situations and people associated with your angry responses. The check list is certainly not exhaustive, but it gives you a start. Once

The Anger Buttons Checklist

Review the list below and circle the numbers beside the people and/or situations that make you angry. Put two circles around those that make you particularly angry.

1 my boss

2 bad weather

3 long line-ups

4 slow waiters

5 the dog (cat)

6 children crying

7 impersonal physician

8 losing a game

9 slow traffic

10 my ideas being challenged

11 feedback

12 my golf game

13 my heart disease

14 losing an argument

15 my children not obeying me

16 having to take medication

17 compulsive talkers

18 politicians

19 juvenile crime

20 my spouse disagreeing with me

> **Manage Anger Effectively**
> **Get Rid Of It**

you have identified the people and situations that tend to get an angry response from you, then order them by degree of intensity. This exercise is necessary to ensure that you develop your anger management program around the most intense issues. You only need a few items to get started, but they have to be genuine ones.........the real anger buttons.

Once you have identified the real anger buttons, you are ready to practice a new way for responding to them. There is one technique in particular that I have found most helpful. It is called self-talk.

Self-Talk: Not Just For Crazies

The self-talk approach requires you to be in tune with your thoughts so as to spot angry thoughts the moment they pop into your awareness. Remember, anger is a direct product of angry thoughts. If you don't have angry thoughts, you won't feel angry. Test it. Try thinking sweet, caring thoughts while at the same time feeling angry. It doesn't work. You need angry thoughts to get angry feelings. So the alternate prescription is rather straightforward. Don't think angry thoughts, and you won't feel angry. It is your thoughts that generate the anger. Therefore, the angry thoughts must be changed if you wish to experience an emotion other than anger. Using self-talk is one way to change them.

Let's take a look at self-talk in action. You are at work. Some creep starts talking to you. You must stay involved because the subject matter is important to you. You don't like this person, and you like what they are saying even less. The feeling of rage sets in fast. Your body stiffens up. You can feel that familiar tightness in your chest. The urge to interrupt, yell, shout, and swear is overpowering.

Now think STOP!

This is a power game with your own mind. Angry thoughts?........
think STOP. A little competition here. STOP wins out. No debate.
No letting anger in for a bit. Anger doesn't get in; STOP enters
the mind. This works when you decide long before any encounter
that mental STOP signals are to rule anger. Anger starts to seep in;
STOP jumps in and takes over the thoughts.

Stop Thinking
Like A 'Mad Man'

Thinking STOP 'hard' is a fast and efficient way, but it may take
you a few steps to get to such a quick method. In the initial stages
you may have to reinforce the thought STOP with more elaborate
images. You may find it helpful to accompany the thought STOP
with an explanatory statement or reminder. For instance,

■STOP .... There has got to be something funny here.

■STOP .... I am not going to let this get to me.

■STOP .... I am getting mad, and it is not going to help.

■STOP .... This situation doesn't mean that much to me.

■STOP .... This is not the end of the world.

■STOP .... Will this mean anything to me next year?

■STOP .... Time to chill. Now remember, calm is fun.

■STOP .... I can't get angry, I'm on an anger management program.

If these reminders are to be helpful, the selected ones must be well
ingrained in your mind so that they surface when you are actually
in the upsetting situation. The trick is to remember them when the
rage starts to penetrate the emotional system. So memorize a few of
your favourites or write them down on index cards. Then they will
come easily to mind when you are under pressure.

This self-talk method seems simple and it is, but it only proves effective
with practice. I still rely on my well-rehearsed self-talk system to do

the job when I start to let anger get the best of me. Lots of practice has taught me to quickly switch gears when anger comes knocking on my emotional door. First step, I say something like "There it is," out loud if possible. This is followed by an automatic mental response that lets my self-talk do its job. It works fast. On nearly every occasion, right on the spot, I bring a more mellow response to the situation or person. No more rage. Of course, I must still deal with the person or situation, but it is always easier because I have control over the emotional response. This is a variation of the old idea that although you may not be able to control all the conditions in your life, you can certainly control your reactions to them. I gain significant satisfaction from being in charge of my response to the situation. Actually, it is quite ego gratifying to gain control over such a destructive emotion. Furthermore, this control has some healthy spin-offs. I no longer feel the need to dominate every person I encounter, or have every situation go the exact way I wish it to. This isn't to say I have given up anger altogether. There are some things worth getting angry over, but now when I get angry it is by choice, not reflex.

Here is a little exercise for you to try once you gain some confidence in your ability to manage anger. This one, when mastered, will get you into anger management college. Most angry people hate to lose an argument So an excellent exercise for you is to allow yourself to lose an argument over an issue that is important to you. Yes, actually set out to lose it. In fact, just the act of trying to lose an argument will be a good experience for you. You will likely find it pretty hard to do on the first occasion, but eventually you will end up laughing rather than getting angry. This little exercise also helps you to realize that most arguments are really not worth losing your temper over. If you keep at it, you may even start to see the humour in some of the situations that heat you up. When that begins to happen, you are really making progress. Most angry people do not see any humour in life's challenges.

Anger's Worst Enemy
A Sense Of Humour

I cannot over-emphasize the importance of learning to control anger. I know it is difficult to come to grips with such a harsh reality in middle or old age. However, it must be done. Anger is a destructive force that puts people in the position of missing out on so many of life's joys because it is incompatible with tenderness, gentleness, relaxation and an overall feeling of well-being. These are the pleasant emotions that await cardiacs once they conquer their anger. It may be a struggle, but it is worth it, and the payoff is fast. Self-talk will prove effective in a very short space of time if you are at the point where you recognize your anger as a problem, and you have managed to identify some of the major situations that trigger it. I know it seems almost too simple to be effective, but let me assure you that if you persist in combating your angry thinking with self-talk, it will not be very long before you are able to maintain your control in a variety of situations that generated nothing but angry responses in the past.

IX
Butts 'n Booze

We have taken a long hard look at the psychological factors that influence your recovery and future heart health. It should now be obvious that the future will be pretty bleak if you don't learn to manage your anxiety and anger. Life becomes a lot easier once you learn to master this 'head stuff.' However, it doesn't make sense to deal with your emotional luggage if at the same time you ignore the physical aspects of your lifestyle. Get real; you had a bloody heart attack! Heart attack.......heart disease.......high risk for death....... yup......it is time to make some changes. Obviously, the psychological changes are essential, but they are not enough. It is also time to take a look at those mundane lifestyle issues like smoking, drinking, using drugs, diet and exercise. I am going to start by encouraging you to examine your smoking and drinking habits. However, before we get into the butts and booze discussion, I want to make a few general observations about health providers and lifestyle issues.

Do not smoke, have no more than two drinks a day, follow a low fat diet, exercise moderately three times a week, and take your pills as prescribed by the physician. I was given those instructions and followed them diligently after my first heart attack. Probably fairly sound advice for as far as it goes. However, it is not a guaranteed prescription for avoiding future heart attacks. It didn't work for me. So I significantly modified the formula following my second heart attack. I have had no coronary events for twenty-five years. Does this mean you should ignore all medical advice? Not at all. It means you should not leave your self-knowledge and common sense at the door of the physician's office.

It would be foolish to assume it is not necessary to make any lifestyle changes after a heart attack. Change is in order, but everyone must find their own equilibrium. I doubt cigarettes in and by themselves are the absolute killers they are portrayed to be by some health promoters. Similarly, a fatty diet is probably not an independent standalone causal factor for heart disease. This does not mean that you should smoke your brains out while you stuff lard down your throat. What it does challenge is the notion that there is a strict linear causal relationship between cigarettes and heart attacks, or between eating excessive amounts of fat and having a heart attack. In other words, no single lifestyle habit is likely to be the sole cause of heart disease. It is more likely that a host of factors, including genetic predisposition, environmental conditions, income, degree of personal happiness, and emotional make-up interact in some complex manner to cause early heart disease.

> **Medical Practice....**
> **Part Science...Part Art**
> **The Bigger Part? Art**

There is no universal lifestyle choice to beat heart disease. Selected lifestyle habits, if followed, merely increase or decrease the probabilities of good health. We all know someone who is overweight, has smoked for fifty years, and is still living a normal life. We also know dead fitness freaks. But hold your sigh of relief. This does not mean you will not have to make any changes, although you don't have to become the medical establishment's perfect cardiac survivor or the health promoter's dream. You are in charge. You have some choices. There is no need to become a health fanatic. Just make some well thought out decisions about your lifestyle. Review your behaviour to determine which habits you intend to eliminate altogether, which ones you will only modify, and which ones are to remain the same. There are no clear-cut answers, but be realistic and recognize that some changes must be made if you intend to avoid an early visit to the grave. I realize most of you are near or past middle age by the time you have a heart attack, so your lifestyle habits have become firmly entrenched over the years. That makes it difficult to accept change. The challenge is significant, but the Cardiac Champ meets it.

> ## Change Can Be Fun....
> ## When You Are In Charge

The need to alter your lifestyle does not require you to turn into a slim, reformed alcoholic who vomits when exposed to the smell of a cigarette. Similarly, you don't have to settle for carrot juice at cocktail parties or step out for five to ten minutes of relaxation twice a day at work. Such intensity is probably a contributing factor to heart disease. Those with such drive are probably at equal risk for a coronary as are the occasional smokers who enjoy a few beers. They are also bores. So lighten up. This is not a journey into the jungle of darkness where continual vigilance must become a way of life. It is not necessary to give up everything you enjoy in your life. Besides, I doubt anyone can give up all the pleasures that the politically correct health promoters deem harmful. Any compulsive effort directed at becoming the medical establishment's 'poster cardiac' is doomed to failure. Take my word for it. Lifestyle changes bring no guarantees, although when you listen to some fitness boosters and read many of the self-help books, it is easy to believe you will live a carefree life until you are a hundred so long as you don't smoke, don't eat fat, over-dose on vitamins, and exercise four times a week.

As I said earlier, between my first and second heart attacks, I adopted the near perfect lifestyle when it came to diet, exercise, moderate drinking and smoking. I worked very hard at following every directive given to me. However, like many post-cardiac treatment programs, the one I followed was not designed to take individual personality factors into account. I didn't smoke, drank very little, followed the perfect diet, exercised a lot, and even did deep breathing. What stress! This rugged regime turned me into a full-fledged anxiety neurotic who worked so hard at not worrying about anything that I ended up worrying about everything.

Nicotine and alcohol are available to most cardiacs around the world. These delights can be helpful in assisting them to cope with the trials and tribulations of life, but they can also create more problems than they solve. The challenge you face is to determine what part you want them to play in your new life as a Cardiac Champ. It would be so simple if there were a formula to follow that guaranteed health, but of course, the reality is something quite different. No cigarettes and two drinks a day is no passport to a long, healthy life. There are simply too many other factors that contribute to good health, not the least of which are your genes. When it comes to lifestyle issues, there are always trade-offs. That means you must make choices.

**Puff, Puff, Puff That Cigarette
Smoke, Smoke, Smoke Yourself To Death**

Got A Light, Mac?

I have had a love-hate relationship with nicotine since my early teens. I smoked fifteen to twenty cigarettes a day for over twenty years. I smoked a pipe for a few years while I was in college. That was considered cool in my day. I also enjoyed cigarillos from time to time after my heart attacks. Like most smokers, I have also spent a lot of time worrying about the effects of smoking on my health. I welcomed in many new years with a solemn vow to never smoke again. I did quit smoking........many times. Ironically, I had been back smoking for only a week, after abstaining for four months, when I took my first heart attack. I began to smoke again a few weeks after being discharged from the hospital. However, after a few months my smoking made me too nervous so I gave it up cold turkey. That time I abstained several years only to start again a little more than a year after my second encounter with death. I continued until recently to enjoy a cigar when golfing and a few cigarettes while drinking with my buddies, but more about that later.

The cigarette has little competition for top billing as public enemy number one in the Western world. Cigarette smoking is condemned by Health and Welfare Canada, the surgeon general in the United States, and most other health organizations around the world. The medical establishment and cigarette manufacturers are locked into a major dispute over the effects of smoking. The past few decades have seen governments and industry spend hundreds of millions of dollars researching the effects of smoking on health. The case against smoking is strong even though there has been legitimate criticism of the research health providers rely upon to justify their warnings against it.[14] Meanwhile, the manufacturers' research claims remain suspect. Neither side has been swayed by the other's research results. Ironically, while the debate goes on, trillions of cigarettes are produced each year as the number of smokers continues to increase around the world. The medical establishment appears to be winning the battle in North America, but losing it worldwide. One thing is certain regardless of the eventual outcome: there will be no final resolution in our time, so cigarettes will remain available

---

14. Johnstone, J. R. and Ulyatt, Chris. *Health Scare: The Misuse of Science in Public Health Policy*, 1991. Australian Institute for Public Policy.
[This small book is an interesting read. Although a bit dated now, it does present a compelling critique of the research cited by health providers to support banning smoking for health reasons.]

to the general public. This means the battle of the butt will continue for cardiac survivors who smoke. All you nonsmokers have already made your decision, so you may wish to move onto the next section. Smokers, we still have some work to do.

The bottom line appears rather straightforward. Will you or will you not continue to smoke, and if you decide to continue how much do you plan to smoke? Maybe the questions are straightforward, but they are difficult to answer, and it can be even more difficult trying to live with the answers. I have no answer for you. You must weigh the pros and cons in light of your unique life circumstances. A Cardiac Champ would review the situation in a balanced fashion, and then make a decision based on his/her own wishes and needs.

There is no sound argument for promoting smoking as good for your health. It seems certain that smoking has some form of debilitating effect on most people's cardiovascular systems since, all things being equal, most smokers cannot perform as well on cardiovascular-demanding functions as nonsmokers. Let's face it. It is highly unlikely that putting such carcinogens into your body over a long period of time will have no ill effects on your overall well-being. However, people do not smoke in a social vacuum. It is only one of many responses that interact with many others in our behavioural repertoire. Thus, the degree of overall harm is relative. For instance, if people stop smoking, but increase their fat intake astronomically and start drinking to extreme, then stop the latter two behaviours once they take up smoking again, the decision as to whether or not they should smoke becomes a little more complex. Similarly, people who decide that they will smoke two cigarettes a day and keep to that regime may be doing less harm, if any, to their physical well-being if the alternative was to experience heightened bouts of anxiety and add two thousand extra calories a day from foods heavy in saturated fats. The broader context certainly complicates the decision-making process.

You may wish to explore the ramifications of this addiction with your spouse or a good friend. It may be helpful to jot down on a piece of paper the good and bad things about your smoking. There may be a number of reasons why you keep smoking. For many people, cigarettes or cigars taste good. They enjoy smoking. Some claim smoking helps them to relax. Many also claim that smoking prevents them from doing other things which they believe would be even worse for their health such as eating to extreme, being continually uptight or regularly showing excessive anger. Others simply think the payoff is not big enough to justify the pain of fighting the addiction. All these may be legitimate reasons for engaging in the activity. However, the positives must be weighed against what you see as the setbacks to smoking. Obviously, you would be crazy to ignore the very forceful, collective opinion of the health authorities whose message is smoking kills. Your smoking may also cause your loved ones significant worry. It may also be a source of worry to you. Besides, this smelly habit really bugs a lot of nonsmokers. As you can see, the issue can be argued from both sides, but a little perseverance and honesty will lead you to the decision that is best for you.

No matter how complex and lengthy the decision-making process, in the end you are left with three choices. Some will decide after careful reflection not to change their smoking regime. So be it. Others will decide to quit cold turkey. Good luck. With cold turkey it takes awhile to reach a comfort zone, but eventually you will probably completely lose the urge to have any cigarettes. The third option is to follow the path of the controlled smoker. These people decide to continue smoking, but set a predetermined amount that they will allow themselves to smoke. This more ambiguous choice warrants further elaboration. Specifically, I wish to issue a few words of caution. A controlled smoking program must be implemented in a systematic fashion. Most of us have a tremendous inclination to trick ourselves when dealing with our addictions. What you must do is review your smoking habit in a thorough and honest fashion. Know how much you smoke and when you smoke. Don't trick yourself. Know exactly how much, when and where you smoke before trying to develop a controlled smoking program. Once you have collected this data, use it to design realistic expectations. Set some very clear and rigid rules if you decide to follow this route. A budding controlled smoker is very vulnerable to self-trickery.

One of your most important tasks is to define moderate. How much, or how little, constitutes controlled smoking? If you are accepting more than fifteen hundred cigarettes a year as controlled smoking, you are fooling yourself big time. That amounts to more than four cigarettes a day. Similarly, six months on, six months off at a pack a day is not moderate smoking. Once you have settled on how many cigarettes you will be allowed each year, then decide if you are going to smoke every day or only in certain situations. I suggest you establish a number of places that are strictly off limits for smoking. Probably your workplace and house are a good idea.

It is very important to never change the limit once you determine how many cigarettes constitute enough. Given your personality, you may respond better to a set limit each day or a set amount for the week, month or even year. Take your pick, but be honest with yourself. If you fall off the plan once, it is probably worth taking another shot at it. However, if you go off the plan a second time, face reality; you are not going to be a controlled smoker. Your choice is now clearer.......are you going to smoke or quit?

> **Thou Shalt Smoke A Little**
> **May Work For Some**
> **Thou Shalt Not Smoke**
> **Is Best For Most**

Earlier I promised to get back to discussing my smoking habit. Well, in my heart of hearts, I wish nicotine had never been part of my life, but that is not my reality. Over the years, it became clear to me that there were definite times when I wanted to smoke, but I couldn't handle being a regular every day smoker. It scared me too much. So I tried to work out a compromise in the form of controlled smoking. For me, it was no longer a question of whether or not to smoke, but how much to smoke. So, about fifteen years ago, I finally settled on a method that was comfortable and seemed to work for me. I know smoking can be harmful, but I figure the degree of harm is a product of the degree of smoking? In other words, there is room for the controlled smoker so long as he can maintain control. That is what I did for awhile. Indeed, I successfully followed a controlled smoking program for several years. I never smoked at work. I did not smoke in my house. I very rarely smoked in front of my children. This regime left me little opportunity to smoke, but enough leeway to satisfy my urges. Sometimes I would smoke at a party or after a good meal, and I enjoyed having a few smokes when I was at the pub with my drinking buddies. I really enjoyed the occasional cigar while playing golf. The only other occasion I smoked was when I was away on a business trip. Unfortunately, my complicated regime included too many exceptions. In a couple of years I started to realize that I was changing the rules as I went along. My career as a controlled smoker lasted maybe two or even three years, before I realized I could not maintain such a strict regime. I opted for total abstinence. I enjoyed smoking, but I came to realize that I was unable to abide by my own controls. So I stopped smoking several years ago. Indeed, I am done with it. This does not mean that I am encouraging all Cardiac Champs to abstain from smoking. Only you can make that decision. However, I must caution the 'wannabe' controlled smoker. The line between satisfying an addiction a little bit and totally succumbing to it is very thin. You must monitor your program with diligence and honesty.

So much for smoking........let's move onto a happier topic.

Everything In Moderation....
Advice Unfit For Human Consumption

Have A Drink Mate

The relationship between alcohol and heart disease or heart health remains a mystery. There is much discussion and substantial research on the subject, but as with most things related to our hearts, there are no clear-cut answers. Not so long ago teetotallers were held in high esteem by the health constabulary. No more. Today, moderate drinking is the in thing. That's right. Drinking in moderation is accepted as a healthy habit. No physician will encourage you to drink in a serious way, but most will accept, or even encourage, drinking in moderation. That means two, maybe three ounces a day. It certainly isn't party time, but at least you won't find too many health freaks pushing the abstinence theme. In fact, some research suggests that teetotallers are more susceptible to cardiovascular problems than are moderate drinkers.

Now for us drinkers, it is no easy task trying to determine how much to drink so that the harm caused will not outweigh the benefits. The research isn't much help. Whatever the amount you decide to drink, you are almost guaranteed that some credible research report exists to support your decision. A long time ago I read about a British study that monitored the drinking habits of twelve thousand male doctors. The outcomes suggested that men would benefit most from a weekly wine intake of almost five bottles. These researchers also claimed that the optimal intake of beer was around two Canadian cases each week[15]. I love them.

Liquor in these quantities is being suggested because of some research claims that alcohol stops the build-up of cholesterol. But is cholesterol your only concern? Even if this amount of alcohol was proven to stop the build-up of cholesterol, you still must consider the other effects of consuming such large quantities. For instance, liver damage and pancreatic inflammation are associated with a consistently high consumption of alcohol. On the other hand, we all know people who have been heavy drinkers for the better part of their adult lives, but still manage to live happy, productive lives without getting cancer or liver damage. They probably end up dying from a heart attack. So once again, the message is a little muddy. If you remove the blinkers, it becomes obvious that as with smoking, there is no universal formula for calculating ideal levels of alcohol consumption.

The last word on alcohol and its relationship to our health remains to be spoken. There are simply too many uncontrollable variables interacting to allow for any universal conclusions. It appears that different people handle the same quantities of alcohol in unique ways. In fact, the individual differences are more notable than the similarities. Furthermore, these differences extend beyond the physical dimension. There is also a great deal of variation among people when you examine the effects alcohol has on their family relationships and work life. Some people can consume a substantial amount of alcohol on a daily basis without it affecting either their work life or their family relationships. Other people who drink

---

15. Canadian Press. Calgary. December 30, 1993.

a similar quantity end up destroying their lives. Therefore, any decisions about alcohol consumption should be personal ones that take into account the social and psychological repercussions as well as the individual physical ramifications.

Most cardiac survivors who are drinkers do not want to give up alcohol simply because they have had a heart attack. However, they may start giving more attention to deciding what is a reasonable amount to drink. There are a number of factors that warrant consideration when exercising this choice. Just like smoking, I suggest you get a plan and stick to it. Sit down with your spouse or a good friend and have a frank discussion about your drinking habits. Try to examine drinking within the context of your overall lifestyle. First and foremost, it is wise to assess the impact your drinking has on your family, social relationships and work habits. If you are drinking to the extent that it interferes with your ability to go to work or to maintain happy relationships at home, then you have a problem. Conversely, some Cardiac Champs use alcohol as a crutch. They find that a few drinks help them to relax or more importantly, give them a break from worrying about their health. Sound like alcohol dependency? Maybe, but not necessarily bad for your health. Alcohol can certainly help one to cope with the trauma of recovery following a heart attack. However, it is important to realize that coping and avoiding is not the same thing. Alcohol may help some Cardiac Champs cope better with their challenges, but it can make some victims avoid dealing with the realities of their heart disease.

> **Alcohol Can Help You Cope
> It Can Also Help You Run Away**

It is wise to consider the possible physical damage heavy drinking can cause even though the effects may not be felt until later in life. In other words, the longer you drink heavily, the more likely you are to experience significant physical problems further down the road. It is also worth noting that alcohol and weight gain are close cousins. Each drink you take means somewhere between a hundred and a hundred and sixty calories. Now if you are an active, fit and trim individual, several drinks a day probably won't have a noticeable effect on your weight. However, if you are rather sedentary and struggle with a weight problem, you will not do yourself any favours drinking six or seven beers a day. You should also remember that drinking booze increases most people's cravings for salty peanuts, fatty chips, pretzels and other junk food. So heavy alcohol consumption may mean heavy doses of salt and fat which may not be advisable for people who are attempting to keep their arterial system in smooth shape. That is why I drink my beer without any of the extras.

I periodically evaluate my drinking patterns with both my wife and friends. I look at it from the physical, psychological and social perspective. I usually have anywhere from two to four beers a day. Occasionally I add a glass or two of wine at supper. This is a fair amount of booze, but the habit, or addiction, has had no adverse effects on my work life or family relationships. I exercise regularly, so it does not pose an unmanageable problem for weight control. Of course, this says nothing about the long range effects such drinking will have on my physical health, although I only missed six days of work during the ten years before I went on pension. What I do know is that in terms of my overall health, this has been a wise lifestyle choice. I thought through the advantages of drinking at a near teetotaller pace, but decided the enjoyment and psychological rewards that accompanied my particular drinking patterns far outweighed what I believed to be the physical risks. However,

I should also acknowledge that I have met Cardiac Champs who drank rather heavily prior to their heart attack, then completely stopped drinking alcohol after it. And these folks are much happier now that alcohol is no longer a part of their lives. So the unique needs of the individual must take precedence over universal rules.

This notion of individual choice is appealing, but you still have an obligation to ensure that your decisions around alcohol are responsible ones in the social sense. You have social responsibilities in terms of family, colleagues, friends and fellow citizens which you must consider when evaluating your drinking patterns. For instance, you have no right to be drinking over the legal limit and then driving a car. Similarly, if your alcohol consumption turns you into a belligerent beast, then you should only be drinking when alone. Lastly, if your drinking wreaks havoc on your children's lives, screws up your work life, or leads you to exhibit antisocial behavioural patterns, then you need to make big changes. Conversely, if you meet your personal and social obligations then the amount you drink really is your choice. Enjoy.

X
Hooked On Drugs

It was a few weeks after being released from hospital following my second heart attack. I was sitting in a cardiologist's office with my wife. By the way, this cardiologist wasn't hiding his displeasure over the presence of my wife. She accompanied me on these visits because most times I was too uptight to hear what the physicians were telling me. This visit was no exception. I was nervous as the cardiologist escorted me into a side room while my wife waited in his office. He took my blood pressure. It registered one hundred and sixty over one hundred. He told me this was too high and would have to be brought under control by medication. I told him that I was very nervous about taking drugs. I was psyched out by the threat of side effects. His only response, "You will be on medications for the rest of your life." It felt like I had just been given a life sentence. I left his office with another prescription.

A few nights later I was sitting in my basement alone. I do not recall a sadder time. I was thinking about all of the drugs I had to take each day. And I was only forty-one! It felt like I was doomed to be a sick junkie for the rest of my life. I got up from the sofa, collected all my pills and set them out in front of me on the coffee table. What a long line-up! There was nitroglycerin in case I got heart pain. There were aspirins. I was taking one every day supposedly as a preventive measure. There was a bottle of Zantac which had been prescribed to treat an ulcer that was probably being aggravated by the aspirin. And now there was Cardizam to treat my high blood pressure, which I wasn't so sure I had, and angina which I had not experienced. Actually I had taken Cardizam when I was in the hospital. At one point it caused my blood pressure to drop so low that they had to start adjusting the dosage. I don't think they ever got it right. There was also a bottle of benzodiazepines (Ativan) which had been prescribed to control my anxiety. Finally, there was another medication to treat the constipation brought on by taking all the other drugs. The only one missing was Lipitor, but it had not yet made an appearance on the market. Once it did I was prescribed it, but I have never filled the prescriptions given to me.

I was having a hard time accepting this sick role. I just could not get used to so many bloody pills. I had never even taken a sleeping pill before my heart attacks. Now sleeping pills were the least of my worries given the line-up of drugs on the coffee table. These were my meds! They confirmed that I really was sick. Obviously, no one takes all these drugs unless they are really sick. It felt like heart attacks and medications were with me for life. My first heart attack had not been so devastating because soon after it I was convinced I would make a complete recovery by simply running my ass off, avoiding fatty food and not smoking. Then the second setback. That threw me for a real loop. There seemed to be no way to recapture my health since a healthy diet, moderate exercise and no cigarettes didn't prevent a second heart attack, with a cardiac arrest thrown in to complicate matters. I had this fantasy where I just kept having heart attacks and going back into the hospital until one finally killed me. I felt miserable. I was thinking like a victim. Looking at all those medications also made me feel like a very sick victim. I started to cry. I am not the crying type, but on this occasion I couldn't help it. However, it proved to be therapeutic. The upset pushed me to start sorting out my feelings.

I stared at the medications on the coffee table for the longest time. I knew the damn drugs were leaving me powerless. I could feel the debilitating effects of allowing myself to be a victim. I craved some sort of empowerment that would grant me a sense of control over my own destiny. Somehow I needed to declare my independence, but I didn't know how to do it. It was the Cardizam that stood out among all the other drugs. I hated that drug. I didn't want to take it. I knew if I started taking that drug I would be at the mercy of the medical establishment for the rest of my life. "You will be on medications for the rest of your life." "Maybe so," I thought, "But it sure as hell will not be Cardizam." I jumped up, grabbed all the medicine, except the nitroglycerin, and rushed into the bathroom. I lifted up the toilet seat, and dumped the works into the toilet and flushed it. I watched the water swirl around, form a tornado-like shape and suck the pills into oblivion. I started to laugh. I was in charge of me.

I am not sharing this experience to encourage everyone to dispense with their prescribed drugs. That would not be wise. I do not believe the dispensing of my medications produced any miracles with respect to my physical health, but I know getting rid of them carried tremendous symbolic significance for me. It represented a turning point because I took back control of my life. I was a Cardiac Champ. The hospital interventions, the rehab therapy, the medications, and the attending physicians were confirming me as a victim of sickness. No more. Now I was in charge of me. That is the key point. Never allow yourself to become a passive victim who has no decision-making role to play in your own recovery. You have the key role even when it comes to the prescribing of medications. It is your body, your mind, your life. Take charge.

You should know, since flushing the Cardizam I check my blood pressure regularly, and it remains in the normal range. The only heart-related medication I have taken over the last twenty years has been the very occasional nitroglycerin pill. You will likely make different choices, but always discuss your drug therapy plan thoroughly with the consulting physician. No medication is without risk, so you must weigh the risk of taking the drug against the risk of not taking it. I followed this approach with one drug and decided to use it over the long haul.

If It Is Going Into Your Body
You Better Know All About It

The Happy Pill Popper

I had never taken a benzodiazepine or sedative in my life prior to my heart attacks. I knew about benzodiazepines because, as a practicing psychologist, I dealt with many people who were taking Valium or Ativan. However, the idea of my ever taking such drugs was out of the question even when I was straddled with persistent anxiety right after my first heart attack. The general practitioner who was caring for me suggested that I take lorazepam (Ativan) shortly following my departure from the hospital. He was a personable physician whose judgment I valued, but I never filled the prescription he gave me. Frankly, I was simply too afraid to purchase the pills and take them. There were innumerable situations over the next three years where the Ativan could have significantly reduced my anxiety. It might even have helped me to get a decent night's sleep. However, my fear of the drug superseded the intensity of my anxiety even though it became so severe I was referred to a psychiatrist. We had one session. He considered the anxiety controllable, but encouraged me to take Ativan for awhile. I refused. When I was in the hospital recovering from my second heart attack, I was given Ativan to help me sleep. I do not recall the exact number of milligrams I took during my stay, but it was no more than one pill on three or four nights. It helped. I was given a prescription for Ativan when I left the hospital. I had it filled at the pharmacy, but spent the next few months debating the risks of using the pills.

A few months after my return home from the hospital, my wife went away with our two children for a week. It was the first time I had been alone since I had returned from the hospital. I was experiencing heightened levels of anxiety. In fact, on two successive days I had terrifying panic attacks. The third day the anxiety was so strong it physically hurt. I had gone several nights in a row with only a few hours of sleep, which made me even more vulnerable. I was ready to do anything for relief. So I took my big lunge into the world of drugs. I went and got the bottle of Ativan and took a milligram. A few minutes later all reason left me. I panicked! I started thinking the worst possible things that were going to happen to me. I remember phoning my wife that night and telling her I was feeling extremely peculiar. I forewarned her that certain disaster was about to strike because I had taken Ativan. She reassured me in her usual calm manner. I felt better so sat down to await the impact. There was no big bang, but it gradually did its work. I slept that night. I took Ativan sparingly over the next twelve years. I consumed between a hundred and a hundred and forty pills a year. This amounted to about a milligram every third day, which obviously did not kill me.

I still experience persistent anxiety from time to time. On those rare occasions, usually in the evening, when anxiety rears its ugly self with its powerful physical symptoms, I will take one milligram of Ativan. I have decided, in consultation with a physician, that moderate use of a benzodiazepine will not harm me as much as prolonged and uncontrolled anxiety. In fact, it offers me an opportunity to relax when it would be otherwise impossible for me to do so. More importantly, it allows me to sleep. This is important, for exhaustion more than anything else can turn you into a victim. The only problem with benzodiazepines is the more you take, the more accustomed you get to them, so eventually you can eliminate their value. However, the drug has not proven addictive for me. I still record each pill I take to keep a record of the amount I consume each year. My dosage has reduced significantly over the years. In fact, for the past ten years, I have been averaging less than a dozen Ativan a year. One cautionary note.....benzodiazepines are sedatives that create drowsiness in most people. Therefore, it is not advisable to combine a benzodiazepine with alcohol or take one when you intend to be driving a car.

Just a few comments about my very periodic use of nitroglycerin. I have taken only two or three dozen tablets over the past twenty plus years. None in the past ten years. Nitroglycerin is a common drug that is prescribed to people who experience chest pain. It can be an effective drug for acute episodes of angina pectoris which can be experienced when, due to arterial blockages, your supply of oxygen is not meeting the demand for oxygen. This creates a pain which nitroglycerin can reduce by diminishing the actual demand for oxygen. Nitroglycerin is a nitrate that relaxes vascular muscles so that you do not require as much oxygen as you do when they are tense. Of course the problem is that many cardiacs, including myself, are never sure if their chest pain is arterially related or the product of being uptight worrying about their hearts. I never seem able to identify the origin of my chest pain, but on a few occasions it has been relatively severe and the nitroglycerin seems to have done the trick. Besides, if I miscue, the nitroglycerin taken as prescribed will not harm me. I don't use any other cardiac-related medications. Many Cardiac Champs take a baby aspirin (ASA) every day as a preventive measure. The only time I take an aspirin is on Monday mornings, but I have no idea why I follow this bizarre ritual.

The Smart Pill Shopper

Let's be realistic. The road to recovery usually requires the cardiac survivor to make some decisions regarding medications because the use of prescription drugs is virtually universal with the treatment of heart disease. Note.......I identify you as the decision-maker. The physician can advise and make recommendations, but you must make the decisions. Some physicians may become a little defensive when questioned about their prescribing habits because the use and abuse of medications is an extremely controversial issue. However, such a reaction should not discourage you from being an active participant when it comes time to determine your drug regime. If you play the role of the passive victim, you do so at your own risk. It is your body, so protect it. No single treatment regime cures all people even when they seem to have similar problems. The interactions and effects of drugs still must be considered within the unique context of each person's body and mind. That requires your involvement. You should thoroughly discuss the proposed drug plan with the consulting physician, and resist the temptation to completely abdicate the decision-making role. This needs to be a team effort, but when it is your body, you should be captain of the team. Here are a few hints on how to be an effective drug captain.

When It Comes To Drugs
The Physician Is Your Consultant
Not Your Manager

Let the physician know that you are an adult consumer who doesn't want to be treated as a helpless victim. Make it clear that you have every intention of taking an active role in planning your drug therapy. This is an important declaration. It helps to prepare the consulting physician for some pointed questions regarding his/her prescribing intentions. Remember, an assertive patient does not have to be an obnoxious one. You can be open and straightforward with most physicians and still maintain a good relationship. The tone of delivery is usually as important as the message. You may say something like this:

Dr. Zorba, I am the sort of person who gets very concerned
over the kind of chemicals I put into my body.
I want to feel comfortable asking questions about any drugs
you prescribe for me.
So please bear with me, and be patient with my questioning.
I want to be an educated consumer so I can properly look
after my best interest.

You may find it difficult to get your little speech out without being
interrupted by the physician. Please appreciate.....people rarely talk to
physicians in a self-assured manner, so they may have their guard up
at the start. Don't give up if their initial response is somewhat aloof
and blunt. A little persistence mixed with patience, understanding
and good humour usually brings them onside. Once you make your
wishes clear, most will try to accommodate them. Indeed, given the
green light, some will even encourage your active participation.

Never enter into a conversation regarding prescription drugs without
a pen and paper because the first step is to make sure that you get
the correct spelling of the drug. The correct spelling of the drug
offers you the opportunity to research it later, and it also puts you
in the position of being able to check the name on the label of the
bottle once you receive the drug from the pharmacy. The physician
will often just say, "Here, you should get this," while handing you a
prescription slip. There is no point in relying on the prescription slip
because many physicians don't write in a legible fashion. It is part
of the mystique.

You owe it to yourself to make sure your temporary vulnerabilities
do not turn you into an ignorant victim. If you plan to take a
prescribed drug, you should know what the medication will do to
you. Ask! What is this drug supposed to do to me? Is it supposed
to thin the blood, stop headaches, open the bowels, prevent pain,

stabilize blood pressure, relax me, or do any other number of things to my body? Be sure you know the expected outcome. You also want to be clear about the side effects of any drug you intend to take. Simply say, "Please explain in detail what is likely to happen to me when I take this medication." All prescription drugs have side effects of some sort. They may be minimal, but you should still be aware of them. Paternalistic physicians may gloss over the side effects fearing you will fall victim to the power of suggestion if they place too much emphasis on the downside. That is, they refrain from focusing on the possible side effects because they fear the mere suggestion will cause you to imagine they are present. There is some validity to this concern, but it doesn't take precedence over your right to know. It is also wise for you to ask the physician what conditions must exist to eliminate the need for taking the drug. Is the prescription a life sentence or is there a way to monitor progress with the hope of stopping use of the drug? You should also know what is likely to happen should you decide not to take the drug. You may get a brusque response to such a query, but it is still an area worth probing. Obviously, if the physician genuinely believes you will be dead in a month if you don't take the drug, that will strongly influence your decision about what to do.

You also have a right to know if the physician has done any independent reading about the drug he is prescribing, or if he is totally dependent on the information provided by the drug manufacturer. If the physician claims to know little about the drug other than what has been communicated by the drug salesperson, then you may wish to consult someone else to get more information. Don't forget, your local pharmacist is probably the best source for getting information on drugs. In most instances, the pharmacist has a more in-depth understanding of the chemicals on the market than does the practicing physician. Conversely, if the physician indicates he has read material, you may ask for a copy of one of the research reports. There is no reason to be snarky, impolite or impatient in attempting to engage the physician in this dialogue. And don't forget, it is always wise to end your consultation with a genuine thank you. Make it clear that you appreciate him/her taking the time to discuss your medication regime with you. It helps physicians adapt to adult-to-helper relationships, rather than victim-to-helper ones, when they receive positive feedback for trying to interact in an adult fashion. Besides, trying to leave the visit on a good note is important because you will likely be seeing the physician again.

Most cardiac survivors lack confidence when it comes to deciding on prescription drugs. That is why so many completely submit to the wishes of their physician. Yet most physicians depend on the drug industry's representatives for much of the knowledge they acquire about the drugs they are recommending for your use. One such example was the internist I encountered following my first heart attack. He put me on Persantine explaining it would reduce the frequency of angina and was even beneficial for preventing future heart attacks. The internist never fully explained the rationale behind his prescription selection, so I never found a comfort level. My apprehension forced me to push for more information from him at each follow-up visit. In other words, I became a general pain in the ass. After a few weeks, he decided to take me off Persantine claiming it was causing me too much stress. I think the move was actually to relieve his stress. Later my research revealed that the Food and Drug Administration in the U.S.A. had never approved the drug as an effective medication for preventing heart attacks.[16] I couldn't even find evidence to suggest that it was helpful in decreasing angina pectoris. The most interesting point? I had not been experiencing any angina following my heart attack.

---

16. Wolfe, S.M. *Pills That Don't Work*, Warner Books, 1981.

My experience should serve as a notice to all cardiac survivors. Be well informed when planning a drug therapy regime with an attending physician. You, like the physician, are unlikely to become an expert on all drugs. However, you must be prepared to interact with the physician as a responsible adult consumer rather than as a vulnerable child. Make no assumptions about your physician's level of expertise on drugs. There are literally thousands of drugs on the market. To get some idea of the number and variety, go to your local library and scan a copy of the *Compendium of Pharmaceuticals and Specialties* published by the Canadian Pharmaceutical Association (2009). Just a quick glance at this drug encyclopaedia will explain why no individual could possibly have even limited knowledge of all the drugs on the market. The sheer volume renders it impossible for any practising physician to devote the time required to acquire such knowledge. Even the drug sales people must confine themselves to areas of specialization, and they devote their entire working life to promoting and selling prescription drugs. So who do the physicians rely upon for information about the drugs? The drug companies' sales representatives. That's right! The sales representatives along with advertising material and publications such as the *Compendium of Pharmaceuticals and Specialties,* which include advertisements from drug companies, are the busy physicians' main sources for information on drugs. There are also the professional journals, but most of them are supported by advertisements from drug companies. In other words, it is near impossible for the physician to escape the onslaught of advertising and promotion generated by the pharmaceutical industry.

This chapter has probably created some concern for you regarding prescription drugs. Good! It is in your best interest to be well informed regarding any substances you are putting into your body. I urge you to use caution. I know medications can play a very useful, and at times life-saving, role in the Cardiac Champ's recovery. However, it is to be emphasized that prescription drugs do not offer any cut and dried solutions. Never fall into the role of victim and leave all responsibility for your well-being with the physician. That would not be fair to the physician or right for you. It is essential for you to pursue a responsible dialogue with the physician when you are trying to determine which prescription drugs to use. You need sound information to make a responsible decision. Neither you nor the physician can work as the lone ranger if you wish to maximize the benefits of medication. It takes a team effort even though some physicians may believe they know what is best for you. In fact, your best interest is rarely served when the physician tries to subtly exclude you from the decision-making process. Do not allow it to happen.

So the message is rather simple. Take an extremely active role in planning the drug regime that you intend to follow. Obviously, the physician is a crucial participant in the decision-making process, but you must never forget that you are an equally important participant. Ultimately the decision as to whether or not you use a prescribed drug is yours, not the physician's. Therefore, it is crucial for you to take the time to think through the pros and cons. As with most important matters, you want to strike a balance. It would be unwise to be so mesmerized by the drug industry's propaganda that you accept any drug put before you. Alternatively, I would not want to see you in the position where your fear of drugs leads you to harm yourself or go through unnecessary misery because of an unrealistic commitment to abstinence.

Enlightened Choice. . . .
Comes With Education

XI
Pass the Salt & Cholesterol

Many cardiacs want to radically change their diets, especially if they have a dietary history that includes substantial portions of animal fat, sugar and salt, but limited amounts of fruits and vegetables. Their spouses are often the driving force behind the diet change. Taking charge of food selection and preparation gives the caregiver a sense of control. As well, putting the focus on diet helps to keep hope alive. "If he just eats the right food, he is bound to live longer." Alternatively, some cardiac survivors use their diets as a tool for denial. They think, "If I just change my diet, this heart stuff will go away." If only it were true.

I am not sure if denial was the driving force for me, but shortly after my first heart attack, I decided my diet required radical surgery. Actually, I became rather neurotic over the whole business of eating. I started my first and only diet project by reading extensively on nutrition, and talking about it even more. This was easy to do because I worked in a public health department where I had access to experts on nutrition and all kinds of reading material. Next, I began to write down every single item of food I ate. I was really worried about the amount of salt, fat and sugar that was in my diet. I wanted a system for calculating the amounts. So I bought food guides that listed how much salt, fat, sugar and calories were in every conceivable food. This was a rather strange obsession for someone who had always eaten three square meals a day and rarely ate in between meals. I liked junk food and probably overdid it with fried foods, but a careful analysis of my diet revealed that it was a relatively balanced one. Nevertheless, several months of faithful recording convinced me that I had to follow a more stringent heart-healthy diet. Big changes were on the horizon. I was hooked!

My wife and I began to take a very thoughtful and deliberate approach to menu preparation. We developed a weekly menu that was characterized by healthy variety and designed to limit cholesterol, fat and sodium intake. I prepared charts to monitor the amount of cholesterol, fat and sodium in the food I ate. I still remember one serving of the shepherd's pie we made included 218 mg of cholesterol, 49 grams of fat and 169 mg of sodium. This contrasted with one serving of our Spanish rice casserole which scored 102 mg for cholesterol, 22 grams for fat and 380 mg for sodium. I eventually stopped eating the Spanish rice casserole fearing the sodium might have a negative impact on my blood pressure. Of course I ran into more grief when I discovered that spaghetti with meat and tomato sauce, although void of cholesterol, had 1066 mg of sodium. There was no winning this game. I turned into a fruit, grains and pasta freak because I was hooked on foods with minimal cholesterol, fat and sodium. That meant lots of oranges, grapefruit, bananas, spaghetti, shredded wheat, honey, strawberry jam (oh, sugar!), and Red River cereal. I went big on pastas because they are low in both cholesterol and fat when compared to meat products. The diet was pretty blah, but there was beer! I knew that beer contained no fat, no cholesterol and only a minimum amount of sodium. So I drank a lot of beer without giving much consideration to what kind of other damage alcohol might do to the human body.

My poor family. They bravely tolerated my fanaticism for over two years, but in the end it just did not work out. It wasn't the food. It was the stress associated with the menu planning, monitoring and food preparation. I began to realize that I could not follow all the rules and regulations governing my plan for healthy eating. Don't misunderstand me. I appreciate that what goes into my body in the form of nutrients, minerals and vitamins is important, but I cannot make a career out of deciding on daily food selections. I learned the hard way that devoting a lot of mental energy to food planning and preparation was not my style. Besides, even with this big effort, I still ended up back in the hospital.

Chubby Wants a Chip

So what the hell are you supposed to do about your diet? There is no simple answer to this question because what constitutes a healthy diet remains open to debate. In fact, it is this ambiguity that has turned nutrition into a big business. There are an incredible number of diets and cookbooks available to the consumer. This means a lot of conflicting information for the poor cardiac survivor who is trying to develop healthy eating habits. Even the popular press is in on the act. It is difficult to pick up a newspaper or magazine today without seeing an article related to diet. The message from the mass media is clear . . . . .'What you eat determines how you look, and how you look determines what others think of you and how you feel about yourself.' The message appeals more to our vanity than our health, but it has left a lot of folks searching for the perfect diet. More than a few people have become millionaires proposing diets that are designed to appeal more to one's paranoia about body image than they are intended to help in the choice of healthier foods.

> **Crash Diets Always Crash**

It seems diet is something everyone holds an opinion on, even though most are based on myths rather than facts. Every diet fad provides its own unique formula for arriving at the perfect weight and maintaining it.[17] Have you noticed how just about every food item at some time or another gets a bad name and is then labelled as a primary cause for some unpleasant disease? It also works the other

---

17. Of course the real bottom line, at least for North America's middle class, is 'we simply eat too much.'

way. Sometimes a food on the 'Don't Eat List' wins approval from some diet guru. Of course, this confusion is very troublesome for the anxious cardiac survivor with an inclination to panic. My only advice is don't sweat the small stuff. You can find your way through this maze of dietary wisdom by following a few simple steps. Start by finding a good dietician. Most modern hospitals have a dietician who will readily see a cardiac survivor. The dietician can review your eating habits with you and make a variety of suggestions as to how you may improve your diet. If you live in Canada, the dietician will also give you a booklet entitled *Eating Well With Canada's Food Guide*. Read it. If you are noticeably overweight, in all likelihood you will also be given a serious pep talk regarding the dangers of obesity. Listen. Now, a food guide and a lecture on weight are helpful, but there are a few more steps on your road to happy eating.

If You Are Obese...
Eat Less....A Lot Less

Once you have seen a dietician, it is time to answer the big question. Do you plan to make any changes to your diet? If the answer is no, move on to the next chapter. If you opt for change, may I suggest you start by taking an honest look at your weight? Get on the scale and don't fool yourself. You don't have to look like a movie star or own the body of a famous athlete, but there is no fun in being the fat kid on the block. This means if you are more than fifteen pounds overweight, it is time to take a systematic look at what you are putting into your stomach. You could start by monitoring your food intake for two weeks. Make sure you mark down everything you eat and, where possible, the exact quantity. You may not get a perfectly accurate count, but after a couple of weeks, you will have enough data for useful analysis. Who knows? You may discover that you eat more quality food than you thought......damn and you are still fat. Unfortunately, the more likely scenario is that you eat a hell of a lot more food and junk than even you thought. So follow through with this monitoring exercise for at least two weeks and discover what you actually do eat.

Fat People Eat Too Much

You have seen the dietician. You have realistically assessed your weight. You have monitored your food intake for at least two weeks. It is time for menu preparation. Let me begin by saying that no particular food can be unequivocally identified as a contributing factor to your heart problems. Similarly, no single food will cure your heart disease. However, your overall diet does have a bearing on your general health, so it may be a contributing factor to what ails you. Conversely, it can be a real asset to your recovery. So when it comes to healthy eating, variety really is the spice of life. It is also worth keeping in mind that the kind of food you select can be as important as the amount you eat. Not all foods are created equal in terms of calories. Fats are sneaky little buggers that carry twice as many calories as proteins or carbohydrates. So deciding what to eat is equally important as deciding how much to eat.

**No One Food Causes
Poor Health Or Good Health**

Relax Fatso

It may be starting to sound as though good food selection and preparation require an unreasonable amount of your time. Wrong. This does not have to become the challenge of a lifetime. Too many cardiac survivors get compulsive about their diets which only adds to their stress. And the stress is probably a greater threat to your health than the lousy diet. The trick is to strike a balance between neurotic vigilance and reckless abandon. Healthy eating stems from a healthy attitude toward food. If you have a healthy attitude toward food, you will recognize the folly of implementing sound eating practices for two months, and then spending six months overeating the wrong foods. You will also stay away from crash diets. As well, a healthy attitude doesn't leave you a miserable and compulsive wreck who spends most of his time planning menus according to Canada's Food Guide. Rather, a healthy attitude toward food encourages you to identify your nutritional goals, and then make food choices and follow eating patterns that reflect them. What you decide to eat is a private matter, but it may be helpful if I share with you how I put my attitude toward food into practice.

If It Takes More Than One Diet You Have An Attitude Problem

I reassessed my attitude toward nutrition after my second heart attack and decided to be less intense. My main objective was no longer to win the acceptance of the Canadian Nutritionists' Association. Slowly I began to realize that I was not committed to following the ideal healthy heart diet in the hope that it would fend off my third heart attack. What I really wanted was to relax and enjoy my food. This attitudinal shift prompted me to redefine my goals.

There is no guru guiding my decision making around food selection, preparation and consumption. In fact, I do not follow any popular diet because I do not believe the road to healthy eating is paved with perpetual diets. I just follow a few homemade guidelines that help me to achieve my four basic goals. What are the four goals? First, I want to enjoy the time I spend on the selection and preparation of meals. This one is easy because I enjoy both grocery shopping and cooking. Second, I do not want to be fat. At my age, I'll accept slightly chubby, but not fat. Third, I want to enjoy my beer. You can pack on the calories with beer so I exercise quite a bit to keep the extra weight off. Lastly, I want to enjoy eating at a restaurant once or twice a week. Here the emphasis is on enjoyment, so I let my taste buds dominate rather than Canada's Food Guide which advises you to, "request nutrition information about menu items when eating out to help you make healthier choices."[18] If I followed that advice, there would be no point to my eating out. Bring on the fries.

I achieve my four main goals by following the nine tips listed below. Maybe they will be helpful to you.

Nine Tips For Happy Eating

1. Have a breakfast fit for a nutritionist.
2. When eating out, make enjoyment the first priority.
3. Avoid processed food.
4. Eat junk food when the urge hits . . . . most times.
5. Eat small amounts at most sittings.
6. Eat lots of fish, fruits and veggies.
7. Go easy on the meat.
8. Avoid salt, refined sugar and saturated fats.
9. Enjoy your beer.

I must be doing something right for my eating habits have kept me healthy and at a reasonable weight for the past twenty years. I think the key is to know yourself, know your objectives, and find an eating pattern that fits with your personality.

I shall resist the temptation to prescribe the perfect diet for the Cardiac Champ. I know what seems good for me may not be good for you, but I guess it wouldn't be much fun reading this section if

---

18. *Eating Well With Canada's Food Guide.* Health Canada. 2007.

I didn't give you some idea of what I eat. So here is an overview of the diet I follow most days. I have always eaten a hearty breakfast. Frankly, it doesn't change from day to day, year to year, or for that matter, decade to decade. I eat half a grapefruit with a couple of prunes on top, hot cereal comprised of small quantities of oat bran, wheat bran and wheat germ mixed with a few raisins, berries and either rolled oats or Red River. I conclude with a piece of toast and honey or peanut butter with a glass of skim milk. A couple of times a week I substitute the hot cereal with a cold cereal such as shredded wheat. Most days in the early afternoon I eat small quantities of fruit, whole wheat bread or rolls with tomato, cucumber, peanut butter or jam as the filler. I cook great dinners of either baked fish and vegetables, varied pastas and vegetables or just a variety of boiled and baked vegetables. Friday is pub night when I generally order whatever appears most appetizing on the menu and wash it down with plenty of beer. I rarely have a dessert with the evening meal, but if I do it is usually ice cream or cookies. I generally do not eat anything in between meals other than fruit. My daily liquids include two or three cups of coffee, a pot of tea, maybe a pop, and a few glasses of beer.

This is not a very elaborate diet, but my liking of fruits and vegetables provides me with enough variety. I do not keep junk food in my house; however, I certainly go out and buy chips or peanuts when the urge hits. To be truthful, I enjoy junk food and can pig out on it with the best of them, so I have to show some control on that front. However, my general attitude toward food, apart from cookies and chips, is that I need it to stay alive. As a result, since I stopped menu planning for heart health, food has not played a big part in my mental life.

If you look in the mirror and like what you see, then you probably are eating the right foods. Nevertheless, it is still essential to clarify what it is you are trying to achieve with your food, and then set out a method that will work for you. If your objective is to follow a diet that conforms as closely as possible to the suggestions of the nutrition experts, then you will have to develop a strategy that follows the directions set down by a reputable food guide such as *Eating Well With Canada's Food Guide (2007)*. Conversely, if you have no desire to follow a standard heart-healthy diet and don't want to make your food choices in any systematic way, then simply go for it. Just make sure you think through all of the options before selecting one to follow.

> ## Are You Really Overweight Or Just Too Short

XII
Run Samson Run

It was ten-thirty on a cold, rainy morning in Edmonton. My body was aching all over. I had been running on pavement for an hour. I was one of the competitors in the Edmonton ten mile road race, a race which I was determined to complete in seventy-five minutes. That meant running ten, seven-and-a-half-minute miles in a row. At the eight mile point my legs were tired, but I had found my pace so knew that I was going to finish and had a good chance of doing so in under seventy-five minutes. Imagine, not even two years since my first heart attack, and there I was competing in a ten mile race. The experience was physically exhausting, but mentally invigorating and a real boost to my morale. I circled the track in Commonwealth Stadium and crossed the finish line in just under seventy-five minutes. I cannot recall many of my thoughts during that race as it was twenty-five years ago, but I do have one clear memory. I remember thinking that I had to be in terrific physical condition since I was able to finish the race. The completed race validated my health. It was a clear sign that I was safe from another heart attack. I was cured. That afternoon I sat soaking in a bathtub feeling pretty confident. Obviously, if I could run a ten mile race, I was a pretty healthy guy. Ten months later, I was on a hospital gurney in cardiac arrest!

Middle-aged cardiac survivors, particularly men, often believe that a strenuous exercise program will bring them to the magic land. They yearn for the feeling of invincibility that comes when they successfully test the limits of their physical capacity. This is partially a physical macho thing, but it is also psychological in that it is directed at building confidence. However, it is a false confidence that rests on a shaky foundation, for it is built on the assumption that a Cardiac Champ is simply a survivor who is physically fit. I do not believe this to be the case. The Cardiac Champ is both physically and psychologically fit and does not need to recklessly push his or her limits.

> # Running Ten Miles Today
> # Won't
> # Keep You Alive Tomorrow

I would never suggest that exercise is unrelated to health, but I do not believe it is a guarantee for good health. I know of people who viewed exercise as a priority, but still ended up with heart disease that killed them. A famous example was Jim Fixx who wrote *The Complete Book of Running* (1977) which sold over a million copies. He was an exercise guru for many Canadians, but died from a heart attack at the age of fifty-two. Alternatively, there are people who shun exercise all their lives, yet manage to live a healthy life to a ripe old age. A very close and dear friend of mine had a desk job all his life and, apart from bending his elbow with a great deal of regularity, avoided exercise like the plague. He lived a robust life for more than ninety years. These contrasts are not only the result of individual genetics. They are also testimony to the fact that health cannot be defined solely in terms of physical fitness. Health is a combination of many factors. The challenge is to determine which particular factors must be present in which combination to maintain good health at the individual level. The variations are endless, so a well-researched self-designed program for healthy living is probably the best bet for you.

Some people believe it is necessary to really sweat it out in order to reap health benefits from exercise. They view pain as a key ingredient for conditioning. This is the 'no pain, no gain' crowd. They are usually attracted to competitive activities such as the racquet sports. You can also see them jogging with gaudy digital watches on their wrists. They glance at their watch at regular intervals to make sure they are running fast enough. Such an obsessive approach to exercising is not recommended for Cardiac Champs. It is a good idea to get in some physical activity a few times a week as it can reap both physical and psychological gains. But remember, you had a heart attack. That means there is something wrong with your cardiovascular system. So if you decide to exercise, take it easy and get some medical advice before designing your exercise program.

If It Hurts...
Don't Do It

Relax. The fitness rage is just about over or at least the push for ridiculously vigorous exercise. We have lived through a couple of decades of aggressive marketing by fitness freaks. However, the fad is starting to wear thin, at least in Canada. In 1985, fifty-three percent of the people in Canada reported doing vigorous physical activity for at least fifteen minutes three or more times a week, but that percentage dropped to forty-seven by 1990.[19] In 2007 Statistics Canada reported that just under half the population over twelve years old didn't even do the equivalent of a half hour of walking each day. It appears as though the 'no pain, no gain' crowd is losing ground to the couch potatoes. Fitness fanatic? Couch potato? Not your kind of role models? Well, consider a third option. Simply bring a more moderate approach to planning your exercise program. This does not mean you should avoid exercise, but maybe you should take a little of the 'vigour' out of it. This is particularly good advice if you intend to make exercise a life-long activity. It is not necessary for you to achieve the conditioning level of a marathon runner. In

---

19.*Canadian Social Trends.* Statistics Canada. No. 31, Winter 1993.

fact, pushing yourself to achieve such heights may be a greater risk to your heart health than no exercise at all. You are not an invalid, but it is still wise to start at an easy pace and gradually work up to more strenuous activities. You should also try to curb any hard-driving tendencies you exhibit while exercising. These include diligent monitoring of time, undue concern with the score, being compulsive about the distance you go, or religiously checking your heart rate. These are all high intensity strategies that do nothing to promote good health. Therefore, if you exhibit these compulsive monitoring behaviours, you may want to develop some counter strategies. I have a few suggestions regarding time and distance that may be helpful to you.

Candidates for Premature Death
Binge Exercisers --- Binge Drinkers

For a start, try to take no notice of time while exercising. This suggestion is particularly relevant to cyclists, runners and swimmers. The cardiac survivors who select these forms of exercise are inclined to measure the worth of their exercise in terms of speed and distance. They become preoccupied with finishing a set distance in a predetermined amount of time. Indeed, many cardiac survivors' personalities make it very difficult for them not to time their exercise to the exact second. They also push themselves to go a predetermined distance in that time. This is not good. It makes more sense to exercise until you get a bit tired or bored, without taking time into consideration. This approach benefits you in two ways. First, you are less likely to overextend yourself. Secondly, it is helping you to modify your personality in a positive fashion by striving to be less intense and goal directed with leisure.

The more intense cardiac survivors also think they must travel a fixed distance that is expressed in a round number. For instance, they find it very difficult to swim forty-seven laps in a swimming pool, but are quite comfortable with forty, fifty or sixty. They can run a kilometre, not fifteen-sixteenths. They need that round number. The urge for such order and predictability keeps everything in high gear; always a goal, a target, an objective. Who needs it! Resist the urge! Try a different approach. The next time you are swimming laps, don't count or if you must count, start swimming forty-one or forty-three laps rather than a tidy number such as twenty-five or fifty. You can also use this approach with jogging. When you are out running, stop part way around the four hundred metre track rather than always running four hundred, eight hundred or sixteen hundred metres. There is no benefit to your being fixated on a predetermined distance, tempo or amount of time. Indeed, it is good for both the head and the heart when you vary your regime. It helps you overcome the compulsive urge to be so precise with your exercise by going a set distance at a set speed at a set time on a given day. This is supposed to be fun. Try to get lost in the pure joy of doing something with no goals. I have brought this approach to my exercise program, and I love it.

Forget The Fitness Levels
Exercise For Fun

After my second heart attack, I came to recognize the value of moderate exercise as opposed to following a strenuous regime. I now realize there is little value in remaining focused on strenuous exercise for its own sake. Swimming is now my exercise of choice during the winter. Cycling and golf are my summer activities. I have been swimming regularly for the past twenty years. I do not make it a very strenuous workout, but it is enjoyable and helps maintain my muscle tone. More importantly, it gives me precious time alone. The key is to be enjoying your exercise of choice, not striving to meet targets. I often swim an odd number of laps just to counteract my own tendencies to approach things in a structured manner. Therefore, I will swim sixty-two, seventy-three, seventy-seven or eighty-one laps in the pool rather than religiously adhering to swimming exactly sixty or eighty laps. Best of all, sometimes I just don't count. That's a tough one for a closet Type-A! I also regularly sabotage my tendency to monitor time, although I must confess that I have cheated on occasion to discover that I can manage a kilometre in less than half an hour. I never measure my heart rate. It just doesn't seem worth it to get all caught up in making sure that I am swimming a predetermined distance within a given time frame so that I can register an athlete's heart beat. Of course, sometimes I do break the rules. Last year I entered an endurance swim competition. However, it was distance over time that counted in this one, so not a risk to my health. A moment of bragging here.......I won it. I just couldn't resist sharing that gem!

I am not suggesting that every cardiac survivor should find the nearest swimming pool and use it two or three times a week. There is a great deal of choice when it comes to exercise, so find an activity you really enjoy. Just choose something, for you are likely to enhance your overall health if you partake in a mildly exerting activity on a frequent basis. Chances are you will also end up enjoying it. And remember, exercise offers an added bonus.......it burns off calories.

> **One Route To Good Health**
> **Aerobic Fitness.....**
> **A Second Route To Good Health**
> **Being Happy.....**

XIII
Don't Think.....Relax

Cardiac Champs usually do well at exercise, but struggle when it comes to relaxation. Most of us are able to flop in a chair or doze on the couch for a few moments of rest, but shutting off our minds or getting a decent night's sleep poses a real challenge. We have all heard the line, "Why don't you just relax? Take it easy," from a loved one. Just relax! It is pretty obvious this messenger has not had a heart attack. You do not just relax after the Big One. That said, the message still makes sense. Relaxation is as important for your well-being as exercise even though most survivors are unable to spontaneously relax their minds, and frequently have trouble sleeping. Sure, we have to shut off the worry once in awhile, but the problem is how to do it. We can't just relax!

> ## Life Is A Journey Toward Death
> ## So What Is Your Rush

It is a mistake to assume that you are automatically gaining the full benefits of relaxation simply because you are not doing anything physical. There is a big difference between inactivity, or a brief respite from physical exercise, and relaxation. Before my heart attacks, giving the ol' brain a little rest was easy. In those days I even used to take afternoon naps. I remember when I lived on the west coast; I would do my gardening, and then stretch out on a lawn chair for an hour letting time pass me by without a worry in the world. My mind was at peace. Now I rarely experience such spontaneous mental breaks. My body tends to get its share of rest, but my mind? That is another story. I must follow a more planful approach to achieve peace of mind.

In the early years following my heart attacks, when there was no external stimulation I would initiate interaction with someone. If that option wasn't available, I would go and exercise or maybe practice putting golf balls on the carpet. Anything to distract myself from worry thoughts. My favourite routine was to do a whole bunch of things at the same time which kept my mind racing at full speed without worry. When I use to travel for my work, I would often sit in my hotel room late at night with my feet up watching television with the radio on while reading the local newspaper with a book I was interested in beside me. At home, I use to engage simultaneously in multiple activities while the rest of the family was playing a noisy game right beside me. Was I relaxing? Well, I know I was not really watching TV, reading the newspaper, listening to the radio or very engrossed in the book. So was I brain dead? No, my mind was alive fighting worry thoughts even though my body was probably getting some rest.

This need to keep my mind in high gear was never a distraction when I was attempting to work, read, write, play my guitar, or do any number of things that required me to concentrate and sit still. In fact, I always have had strong powers of concentration when engaged in a demanding activity. It is passive mental activity that can leave me with worry thoughts. However, over the years I have found ways to significantly limit such thoughts, if not get rid of them. If you share this problem, don't try to rationalize it away by concluding, "I can't relax, but so what......who really needs to relax?" A healthy lifestyle has to make room for quiet moments that are characterized by both the body and mind being still. Everyone needs time to relax, but if you are like me, it may take some innovation to meet your relaxation needs. I look at my heart attacks as a death sentence when it comes to spontaneous, mental relaxation. The important word to note is spontaneous. I can get mental rest, but I have to prepare for it.

Peace of mind is hard to achieve when the idea of your heart going crazy is lurking in the subconscious most of the time. Such a morbid threat makes it very unlikely that your mind will spontaneously shift into cruise control. However, although it may take some time, you can learn to put your mind at peace. Many people successfully gain this inner peace by learning to meditate.

Going Weird

The mere mention of the word meditation conjures up weird images for many cardiac survivors. Meditation calls for a passive, but receptive attitude that doesn't come easily to the usually pumped-up cardiac. We tend to be action-oriented folks who concentrate on work-related activities, achievement and competitive forms of recreation. I was certainly not impressed when first introduced to meditation. All I could picture was some guru sitting on top of the Himalayas for two or three hours every day contemplating the purpose of the universe. That is not my idea of having a good time. However, I soon discovered that even if such gurus do exist, you do not have to become one to reap the many benefits of meditation. So don't let the common stereotypical image prevent you from gaining a very positive experience. Even though many of the books written about meditation leave the reader thinking it is an extremely complicated business, you can gain the benefits without getting overly complex. Let me explain.

Give Your Mind A Rest
Meditate

The goal of meditation is rather straightforward........achieving the temporary absence of thought while you stay awake. What makes meditation unique is that you reach your goal not by doing, but rather by 'not doing.' Thus, meditation involves stillness of the body and mind. In a nutshell, the idea is to sit still for fifteen or twenty minutes with a blank mind. This is no simple feat, but you can come ever closer to achieving it with consistent practice. It is certainly no more difficult to learn than playing golf sufficiently well to consistently crack a hundred.........another dream of mine.

Why don't you start practising right now? Here are a few pointers that will help you attain stillness. Start with the body. A person can meditate sitting on the floor, lying in bed or sitting in a chair. I do not recommend trying to meditate in bed because you may end up falling asleep which is not the goal here. Some may opt for sitting on the floor. In eastern cultures, the cross-legged lotus position is ordinarily used, but it is difficult to do. It requires you to sit on the floor and cross your legs so that your right foot rests on your left thigh, and your left foot rests on your right thigh. This position demands a fair amount of flexibility. I have never managed to twist my body into this shape so I always use a chair. If your choice is a chair, then the first task is to find a comfortable one. A proper chair allows you to rest your feet flat on the floor when your bum is up against its back. Here is the way you should settle into the chair.

- Place your feet flat on the floor twelve to eighteen inches apart.
- Let your shoulders relax which means they will be slumped slightly forward.
- Make sure your lower back is straight.
- The head should be erect, but not stiff.
- Place your hands on your lap with the back of your left hand resting in the palm of your right hand. Alternately, you may wish to place your hands on your thighs with the palms up.
- The eyes remain open, directed a few feet in front of you. Don't try to focus. Just look out.

Once you are positioned in your chair this way, you should wiggle and squirm a bit until you feel relaxed and comfortable. If the chair is comfortable, most people will not find it difficult to establish this position and remain relatively still for a moment. The challenge is to remain still for more than a moment. This takes practice, but if you persist eventually you will be able to sit in this position, perfectly still, for fifteen or twenty minutes.

Turning the mind off is not so easy. The idea of not thinking is really alien to most of us, so learning to stop our thoughts is tough. We think, think, and think from the moment we wake up until the time we fall asleep. Even in our sleep our minds are actively at work creating the images for our dreams. It seems weird to be searching for a way to turn the mind off particularly when we are not supposed to use the mind to accomplish this goal. It appears to defy logic because the whole idea is to avoid trying to blank out thought, prevent distractions, or evaluate our lack of progress, yet that is precisely what we want to do. However, it starts to make sense when you learn a few simple mental exercises to help you overcome possible distractions.

I Think...
Therefore I Worry

The most common technique for helping people to meditate is to have them focus on their rhythm of breathing. Once you get comfortable in your chair, turn your attention to your breathing. As you inhale, trace the voyage of the air through your nose, then down your throat, into your lungs, down your chest, and into the depths of your stomach. Similarly, as you exhale concentrate on feeling the air leave your stomach; come up through your chest and out your nose and mouth. Some people enhance their focus with repetitive mental counting. That is, they think in slow motion the number one as they inhale, and then slowly think the number two as they exhale. They mentally repeat these two numbers in rhythm with their breathing pattern. I have never been able to achieve the focus required for this kind of mental counting, but I know people who find it the most effective way to set their minds at peace.

There is a second exercise for gaining mental serenity that I find a lot more helpful. It involves shutting down my mind by focusing on a nonsense word which I discipline myself to continually repeat in a rhythmic fashion. The word without meaning is called a mantra. It is important to ensure that the mantra blends in easily with the rhythm of your breathing and conjures up no other word associations. That is why it is best to select a nonsense word. Obviously, if you are a school teacher, book is not a good mantra. Similarly, hammer is not a suitable mantra for the carpenter. The best selection is a two-syllable sound that has no meaning. I prefer the idea of a two-syllable sound because it allows me to repeat one syllable while inhaling and a different one while exhaling. It is not as effective to repeat the mantra in an unrhythmic fashion so make sure it is in unison with your breathing. One syllable while inhaling and the other syllable during the exhale.

Some people find it necessary to have several mantras available because once they get used to focusing on a specific mantra, they seem to get a lot of interference at the mental level. This has not proven to be the case with me, but if it works for you, then have several mantras. I have used **razz......mahhh** as my mantra for years, and continue to find it a very effective one. Actually I repeat the sounds mentally rather than saying them aloud. I sense the sound 'razz' as I am inhaling and the sound 'mahhh' as I am exhaling. These two sounds do not conjure up any images for me, so my mind remains free from all problems, fantasies, and plans. Thinking my mantra in a repetitive fashion also helps me to avoid problem solving and other mental gymnastics.

I don't think any cardiac survivor should ignore this opportunity to be void of all thought. It is so peaceful to be engaged in an activity with no demands. You are not trying to think of anything, but you don't have to bother fighting your thoughts. Even when distractions do enter, they are allowed to rest there until you become aware of them; then you can passively return to your mantra without making any sort of evaluation of your progress. In due course, it comes to be a nondemanding experience that leaves you feeling calm, replenished, and looking forward to the next time you can sit down to meditate. I realize this form of meditation is not designed to lead you into tremendous insights about yourself or the world. Similarly, it is not going to help you discover the unknown truths about the universe. However, if you start with ten or fifteen minutes of practice each day, you will soon discover it offers a kind of peace that you will look forward to experiencing each day. Try it!

> **An Idle Mind
> Breeds Contentment**

Time For A Snooze

I was in bed at 11:30 p.m. It is now 2:30 a.m. I am still awake. I have a T-time at 7:40 a.m. Many cardiac survivors know this feeling. Even if you were a good sleeper in the past, it is quite possible that you will find it difficult to sleep after you have had a heart attack. Alternatively, if you were a poor sleeper prior to your heart attack, you will likely be a worse one after it. Mind you, not every cardiac survivor ends up an insomniac. Nevertheless, insomnia is a common problem even among Cardiac Champs, although most learn to live with it. The key to such an adjustment is learning to accept insomnia as an inconvenience rather than a tragedy. This attitude is essential if you are to maintain your sanity because insomnia can become a nightly horror if you let it get the better of you. Obviously, I suggest you find a way to live with it.

I had been a minimal sleeper since my late teens, but real insomnia only set in after my first heart attack. However, I have gradually learned to live with this inconvenience after years of practice. My journey of adaptation passed through three distinct stages. The first was the longest and most brutal. It lasted from the time of my first heart attack until a few months following my second one. I spent most nights during this period worrying about my health, my work, my future, and any other number of things that would keep the average person awake. This was also the time during which I desperately struggled to understand and cope with my panic attacks. I rarely, if ever, got a decent night of sleep.

I directed all of my nighttime energy at fighting anxiety. I was determined to beat it. Early on in the battle I decided that I would not get up and spend the night pacing around or sitting in a chair counting sheep. I believed such avoidance of my bed would produce increased anxiety. So I would spend the entire night with the lights out lying in bed awake. I was getting plenty of exercise as I twisted and turned for hours each night. Fortunately, this nightly ritual was not disruptive for my wife. Like so many Cardiac Champs, I married a calm, optimistic, confident person who has no interest in spending the wee hours of the morning worrying about trivial matters. She sleeps like a log. I roll like a log. It was not unusual for me to spend two or three consecutive nights fighting off panic attacks and trying not to worry about my heart. I took no sleeping pills or benzodiazepines during this time, and sought no relief from alcohol. Many mornings

I would get out of bed after lying awake all night. I doubt there was even one night when I got more than four hours of uninterrupted sleep. I often found it very difficult to navigate through the day as I was suffering from complete exhaustion. This created additional worry as I wondered about the ramifications so little sleep had for my overall health. This hell lasted for three years!

The second stage of my battle with insomnia began a few months after my second heart attack and cardiac arrest. I was still spending most of my nights awake, but gradually the intensity of my worry began to reduce. This coincided with the new attitude I was developing in response to my health condition. I was feeling a lot more confident, which reduced my overall concern about death. This meant a lot less anxiety at bedtime. However, my sleep patterns remained erratic. My new found confidence led me to declare open war directly on my insomnia. What a mistake! The new found confidence and determination were a good sign, but the wrong ammunition for fighting insomnia. I found myself spending hours 'trying' to go to sleep! I would count sheep, lie perfectly still and repeat a mantra, monitor my breathing, say the times table, or try any other technique I thought would help. I would virtually work myself into a turmoil by spending night after night ordering myself to get my act together, stop thinking and go to sleep. It became a real battle. Never one to give up, I stubbornly persisted at trying to find a way to stay asleep for six or seven hours. This never happened. I would sleep a few hours, wake up, fall back to sleep for short periods of time, and then wake up for the day sometime between 4:30 and 5:30 a.m. This pattern continued for a couple of years. My lack of success created significant frustration and tension. I had replaced my anxiety with frustration and anger. The whole battle exhausted me.

The third stage brought me peace because I finally gave in to my erratic sleep patterns. I slowly began to recognize that for whatever reason, I was not a person who was going to go to bed at 11:00 p.m., be asleep before 11:30 p.m., and wake up the next morning well rested after seven hours of uninterrupted sleep. Nights of prolonged deep slumber are simply not in the cards for me. I do not know why this is the case, but my acceptance of this reality has brought a significant degree of peace and tranquillity into my life, or at least into my night life. Now when I am tired I look forward to going to bed. I know I will not be spending six or seven hours in a deep sleep, but I anticipate a restful time. I guess my body does not require seven hours of sleep each night. In fact, I do not seem to need more than four or five hours most nights. I am able to function at full capacity so long as I manage to get around five hours of sleep sometime between midnight and 6:00 a.m. Since I stopped work, if need be, I also take an extra hour or so lying in bed resting while awake. An afternoon power nap is also not out of the question. Ah, the joys of retirement.

Some nights I am unable to sleep much more than an hour or two, but I have learned to live with this reality, although I do feel the effects the following day. When I was still working if I experienced two sleepless nights in a row, I would take a milligram of Ativan the third night. That guaranteed me at least five hours of uninterrupted sleep. I used Ativan sparingly, so I remained quite responsive to small doses of the drug. Now that I am retired, I am able to make up for any lost sleep simply by resting in bed longer in the morning or taking it easy during the day. The important lesson to be learned here is, don't fight your insomnia. Accept it as just one of those minor irritants people have to put up with in life. Who knows? You may even get a bit more sleep with that attitude.

It is also helpful for you to have some techniques available for relaxing your body. Your partner will appreciate this as it will stop you from fidgeting after the lights are out. It is common to experience muscle tension when you are lying in bed awake for extended periods of time. Some people avoid this by getting up and pacing around the house, watching late night TV, or raiding the refrigerator. I believe these techniques simply delay the inevitable, so I lie in bed and take whatever relaxation comes my way. Sometimes I help the process along by using meditation techniques. For instance, an easy way to relax your body is to concentrate on your eyes. Close your eyes and think of the eyelids being very relaxed. If you concentrate on your eyes and start to relax your eyelids, usually the state of relaxation will extend to other parts of your body.

Another way to relax your body is by practicing a condensed form of systematic muscle relaxation. Lie in bed and systematically concentrate on tightening and releasing the tension in your various muscles. Start with your feet and work up to your forehead by tightening and relaxing each muscle group in turn. This method can also help shut down your mind because the concentration it takes to focus on your muscle groups diverts you from troubling thoughts. However, I must confess, I find muscle relaxation techniques too exerting for the middle of the night. Besides, if you have accepted the idea that your time in bed is essentially for lying down and taking what comes, then your body will relax on its own.

Insomnia is difficult to conquer, but following the above suggestions should prevent it from becoming a major psychological problem.

The key is bringing an accepting attitude to bed with you. Get into bed, stretch out, and enjoy whatever the night brings. Recognize that insomnia does not spell disaster. Sooner or later, your body will take the rest that it needs. You do not have to make getting to sleep the number one priority in your life. Look at bedtime as a time to relax and enjoy even if you do not sleep. It can be very enjoyable getting cosy and comfortable in your bed while filling your mind with pleasant thoughts, not for the purpose of helping yourself sleep, but simply for the sheer enjoyment that accompanies happy thoughts. Your thinking can be relaxed, varied, nondemanding, and all over the map. Let yourself enjoy this time when there are no demands on you.

XIV
A Final Word

The Cardiac Champ's number one question is not, "How long am I going to live?" but "What am I going to do between now and the time I kick the bucket?" Keep it simple here. You gain nothing by letting a past heart attack get in the way of having a good time now. You are no invalid. There may be some restrictions placed on you because of your heart disease, but that doesn't mean fun must be taken out of your life. In all likelihood you can still visit with friends, go to the theatre, play and listen to music, sing, have sex, laugh, write, paint, read, love, sit still, watch nature, play games and do some exercise. Some lifestyle changes are in order, but you are still in charge of the attitude you bring to these new conditions.

Yes, you had a heart attack, but this does not mean it is time to enter a protective shell where you view nearly all activity as a challenge to your heart. It doesn't make sense to resign yourself to a life of perpetual worry. An overprotected worry wart is virtually paralyzed when it comes to having fun. Sure, you had a heart attack, but remember.......you survived it! Yes, chances are if you have another one, the lights will go out for good. So what? The fact is you may live for six months, six years, or sixteen years. Right now, that sixteen years must seem pretty unrealistic, but just think, I am still going strong twenty-five years after my second heart attack and cardiac arrest. There is no way to predict how long you are going to live. However, I can assure you that if you give up, feel sorry for yourself, moan and groan, and engage in other pessimistic activities, you certainly will not enjoy whatever time you do have left.

The big challenge is learning how to live a full, happy, active life once you have left the hospital. It is quite likely your heart disease means your time is more limited than it would have been without it, but don't fret. Take full advantage of whatever time remains. Remember, just because you have had a heart attack, it doesn't mean that all future activity must be directed at improving your heart health. The zest goes out of life when you make the creation and maintenance of a healthy heart the central purpose of your existence. Be kind to yourself. Spend a couple of hours every day doing what makes you feel good. There is no substitute for enjoyment.

**You Only Go Around Once....
Make Sure You Have A Good Time**

The real threat of heart disease is the potential damage it can do to your attitude. It is attitude that separates the Cardiac Champ from the ordinary survivor. You will make a grave mistake if you interpret your medical history as a sign to leave the world of play to become a serious, diligent observer of your illness. There is nothing to be gained by deciding that you are unable to be active because you have heart disease. Cardiac Champs are the ones who develop the confidence to live an active life in spite of their cardiovascular shortcomings. They reject the role of victim, make the required lifestyle adjustments and get on with enjoying life. Cardiac Champs, more than anyone else, recognize the importance of making every moment count. They know the real threat is not premature death, but losing the ability to have a good time while alive.

No two cardiac survivors will walk down the exact same path. We must all find our own road. I certainly do not have the precise formula for turning you into a Cardiac Champ. However, so many people ask me about the main principles or attitudes guiding my lifestyle that I feel obligated to share the major ones with you. You will quickly note that most of the principles guiding my lifestyle choices relate to psychological and social issues rather than physical ones. This reflects my belief that the key to living a healthy, vigorous, happy life after a heart attack depends much more on attitude and emotions than on eating, smoking and exercise habits. So for whatever it is worth, here is this Cardiac Champ's credo.

- Get to know your real self, and get to like you.

- Make room in your life for the people you love.

- Don't get angry, don't get mad, and don't get even.

- Find humour wherever it hides.

- Laugh...........laugh a lot.

- Don't make giving up bad habits your primary purpose in life.

- Identify the lifestyle changes you must make; then make them.

- Start the day with a hearty breakfast fit for a nutritionist.

- Eat a lot of fruit, fish and veggies. Beer is on the menu too.

- Benzodiazepines can help, but carefully monitor their use.

- The only exercise worth doing is that which is fun.

- Don't sweat the small stuff.

- Learn some effective relaxation techniques.

- Take a few risks. It helps to avert boredom.

Now Go Play!

CPSIA information can be obtained at www.ICGtesting.com
Printed in the USA
LVOW070752280712

291889LV00017BB/41/P